James and Portia Davis, 1983 • Grapevine section, Madison County, NC

The Face of Appalachia

The Face of Appalachia

PORTRAITS FROM THE MOUNTAIN FARM

TIM BARNWELL

FOREWORD BY GEORGE TICE • PREFACE BY SAM GRAY

W. W. NORTON & COMPANY • NEW YORK • LONDON

The Face of Appalachia: Portraits from the Mountain Farm
Tim Barnwell
Copyright 2003 by Tim Barnwell

Manufacturing by Mondadori Printing
Book design and composition in Electra by Katy Homans
Production Manager: James Mairs

Library of Congress Cataloging-in-Publication Data
Barnwell, Tim 1955-
The face of Appalachia: portraits from the mountain farm / Tim Barnwell.
p. cm.
ISBN 0-393-05787-9
1. Appalachia Region, Southern—Social life and customs—Pictorial works.
2. Appalachia Region, Southern—Social life and customs. 3. Mountain life—Appalachian Region,
Southern—Pictorial works. 4. Mountain life—Appalachian Region, Southern. 5. Mountain people—
Appalachian Region, Southern—Pictorial works. 6. Farm
Life—Appalachian Region, Southern—Pictorial works. 7. Farm life—Appalachian Region, Southern.
I. Title.

F217.A65B38 2003
975.6'8'0222—dc21

W. W. Norton & Company, 500 Fifth Avenue, New York, NY 10110
www.wwnorton.com

W. W. Norton & Company Ltd., Castle House, 75/76 Wells Street, London, WIT 3QT

IDENTIFICATION OF PEOPLE IN GROUP PHOTOGRAPHS

Following is a list of people appearing in group photographs who are not identified in the image title.
Names are arranged as the people appear from left to right in the image.
Page 32: Stephanie and James Burnette, Jr., James Burnette, Sr., Larry Norton; page 33: Anita, Tammy, Joe,
and Roger Davis; page 35: Melinda, Sherry, Douglas, and Lela Ramsey; page 37: Arnold Gosnell, William
Roberts, Glenn Price, Alan Rathbone, Dwight Roberts, Robert Roberts, Ben Gahagan; page 40: Johnny
Coates, Ganell Clark, Floyd Coates, Vance Ingle; page 48: Terry McDowell, William Robert Singleton,
Johnny Wood, Darin Hullender; page 67: Janie and Roxanne Hylton, L. D. Fender, Lindsey and Phyllis
Bradley, unidentified son and mother, Jessie Fender; page 74: Eddie Payne, Gary Frisbee, N. Plemmons,
Kevin Meadows, Rex Meadows, Stevie Frisbee, Harold Scott, Dwight Meadows; page 91: Beth Turner,
Tina Coates, Belinda Aiknes, Rachel Bradley, Tina Robinson; page 109: Randle, Timothy, Robert, and
Jolly Mae Collins, Jackie Fox.

Cover: Collie Payne and steer, Berry, in tobacco field, 1981 • Big Pine Creek, Madison County, NC

Contents

Acknowledgments

I would like to thank my wife, Kathryn, for her unwavering support of my work and for understanding the long hours involved in both completing this project and bringing it to book form. A special thanks goes to my daughter, Callie. Born several years after I began this project, she has grown up around it, and has been a great help in preparing the book materials. To my friends Steve Mann, Tad Stamm, and especially Nick Lanier, I am indebted for their invaluable assistance in all phases of this project. I would also like to extend my gratitude to Jan Oliver Alms, for his countless hours in the graphic design of the many book prototypes, and to Gary Singleton for numerous introductions, and his company on trips early in this project. Many thanks to George Tice, an ardent and longtime supporter of my work, for his advice, knowledge, and assistance. To all the folks at W. W. Norton and Company—my editor James Mairs, editorial assistants Catherine Osborne and Brook Wilensky-Lanford—and to book designer Katy Homans, I am greatly indebted. Although it is impossible to thank all the people who have helped in the course of the last twenty-five years, and I apologize to anyone I may have omitted, I would like to extend my heartfelt appreciation to the following people: Virginia and Harris Campbell, Howard and Alice Barnwell, Ken Lawson, Ralph Burns, Richard Dillingham, Dr. John Killian, Phyllis Genetti, Carson Graves, Judy Canty, Brigid Burns, Johnny and Lockie Coates, Sam Gray, Robert Brunk, Michael Sherrill, Sally Stark, Steve Brechbuhl, John Cram, Ernest Teague, John and Phyllis Smith, David Chalk, Rob Amberg, Marlitia Gault Correll, Pete Smith, Richard Hasselberg, Rita Hayes, Jerry Plemmons, Don Pedi, Mary Douglas, Ruth Summers, and Cole Weston.

FOR MY FAMILY

B. W. Payne family working hay, 1981 • Little Pine Creek, Madison County, NC

Preface

Western North Carolina and Eastern Tennessee, like much of rural Southern Appalachia, are places where topography has contributed to a strong local identity. It is, and has been for many generations, a country of farmers, burley tobacco, cattle, copious gardens, steep slopes, durable traditions, and hard-working families. On the timbered flanks of the Walnut and Bald Mountain ranges and in the deep soil fertility of the coves and bottomlands along the tributaries of the French Broad River, ancient patterns of labor, rest, and relation took hold in the rich earth as English-speaking families settled there in the late eighteenth century.

For the next century and beyond, the southern mountain region was comprised of frontier enclaves surrounded by more urbanized centers—Atlanta, Asheville, Knoxville, and Roanoke. These rural mountain communities endured and often prospered. Their ways upon the land— the patterns of living and working, the songs and stories they shared—lasted, with little change, well into the twentieth century.

Their "otherness" assured that they did not lack for curious outside observers, whose text, drawings, oral histories, and photographs leave us documentary legacies of a way of life characterized by straightforward joys, hardships, isolation, and independence. Working in or around Western North Carolina in the first decades of the twentieth century, photographers Doris Ulmann, Margaret Morley, Bayard Wooten, and William Barnhill, among others, left collections of photographs that vividly convey the textures of mountain living.

Tim Barnwell's careful, consequential work is solidly in this tradition. It demonstrates a capacity to look steadily and unobtrusively into the working lives of rural people whose relation to the land and way of life is often inscrutable to the modern urban mind. Tim's work is suffused with a generosity of spirit that resonates with the generosity of the people he spoke with, got to know, and photographed.

Once, conversationally, Tim addressed the linguistic tropes of "taking" or "shooting" pictures. "I don't want to *take* photographs, I want to *give* them," he said. I believe this ethic is an essential reason for the intimate quality of Tim's images. The people, their work and repose, strength and fragility, their tools, land, and animals are quietly present as sacred gifts exchanged between subject, photographer, and reader.

Now, the indigenous culture of the steep Appalachian hills is changing more rapidly than at any time in history. Since Tim began documenting mountain life and work a quarter of a century ago, a steady influx of retirees, developers, young urban escapees, migrant workers, and new highways have steadily altered the land, local identity, and the demographics of the area.

Tim Barnwell's photographic gifts help us understand and assimilate these changes. They remind us of ancient truths and a kind of beauty that seems, more and more, to be obscured by the noise and movement of a world in pursuit of its future.

SAM GRAY

Amos Henderson and pet chicken, 1982 • Lonesome Mountain, Madison County, NC

Foreword

Tim Barnwell's *The Face of Appalachia*, *Portraits from the Mountain Farm*, is filled with so many great photographs (and I do mean great), that further editing would prove not only difficult, but painful. There are no expendable pictures here. When an artist has as many remarkable images as he has, we can truly praise him. Great photographers make great photographs.

He has been gathering these images and text for most of his adult life. Not many photographers could sustain that kind of ambition for twenty years, and more. If this book had been published ten years ago, it would be less than it is, but he has given it time, refined his ideas, perfected his craft, and guided the work to completion.

He approaches his subjects by getting to know them, gaining their trust before he photographs them. When they are ready they look directly into the camera. They strike their own pose, giving their portrait to him. To that end, he is supremely successful.

And then, we hear their voices as they tell their stories. He puts them at ease. He draws them out. They didn't know they were saying anything of consequence; it was just talk. Tim knew differently. What they say is of the utmost importance to him. Later he would shape it into prose.

Listen to Amos Henderson of Lonesome Mountain worrying about the well-being of his one-legged chicken. Look at the unforgettable photograph of him holding his pet as one might tenderly hold and support an infant, and you will know something of love.

Clyde Massey had to have seen the same Roy Rogers movies I did to have named his faithful horse Trigger. Maybe Clyde dreamed of being a Hollywood cowboy in his youth. Who knows? And Bob Roberts with his unnamed dog is another prime example of man and his relationship to his animals.

Examine the photograph of Byard Ray. Could it possibly have been composed better than it is? Within its modest and fragmentary frame is a complete and perfect portrait, the very essence of the man. See Fred Barnett, deep in thought, searching his memory, perhaps for an answer to a question posed. Some future seer might be able to read his mind. Whatever he was thinking about was a long time ago.

Look at Kate Church; she looks as worn as the mop next to her. She might be younger than she appears. If so, you know she has had a hardscrabble life, much of it spent outdoors. But she looks happy and grateful for the attention paid her.

Barnwell's masterpiece might be the photograph of Peggy Harmon tending her dying aunt. They gaze into each other's eyes, as the younger woman comforts the older, brushing the hair from her face. I'm reminded here of W. Eugene Smith's famous photograph "Tomoko in her bath." It has that same kind of power—the power of love.

A lot of Tim's love has gone into this book—a love of the land and those who inhabit it. If these people are shaped by the land (and they are), Tim Barnwell grew out of the same earth. By immortalizing them, he has immortalized himself.

GEORGE TICE

Alice Davis sitting on porch, 1983 • Grapevine section, Madison County, NC

Introduction

The photographs presented here are the culmination of more than twenty-five years of personal photography. They are, in part, my attempt to document the vanishing way of life of the mountain farmers and craftspeople. While the rural landscape has always been a central theme in my photography, I formally began this endeavor in 1977. I was twenty-two, had just graduated college, and was working as a photographer for *Mountain Living* magazine, a regional publication based in North Carolina. After a conversation with the editor about my fascination with traditional mountain life, she assigned me to produce a feature article on the subject. This launched an adventure that took me into the remote regions of southern Appalachia and provided an introduction to some of the most extraordinary people I have ever met.

I have always been intrigued by the habitat that people create over a lifetime and the relationship between the land and the people—how each shapes the other. I felt that combining environmental portraits with landscapes would best convey the character and sense of place of this unique area. This project enabled me to explore these ideas. After the article was published, I continued to work on my own. Whenever I could get a day free, I would load my 4 x 5 view camera, tripod, and a backpack of film holders into my four-wheel drive and explore the back roads, stopping whenever I found a compelling scene or a willing subject. I would spend as much time as possible with each person before making photographs—learning about them and hearing stories from their lives. As I began to share these images, I found that people enjoyed the stories as well. When exhibiting the work, I started including excerpts from the conversations I had with each person. These text passages added an important dimension to the project, and I have incorporated them here as well. They start on page 118 and are coordinated to the images by each subject's name and location.

The most common questions I receive about the images are, "How did you find these people?" and, "How did you get them to let you take their picture?" In answer to the first question, our family lived in Marshall, a small town in Madison County, North Carolina, in the 1950s. My father was a teacher and football coach at Madison High School and my mother taught at Walnut Elementary School. Later, my mother remarried and was living in the county again when many of these images were made. Although I knew the area well, most of the people I photographed were strangers whom I met where they lived or worked. This proved to be quite challenging for me, as I had never been very outgoing growing up. While fairly comfortable with people one-on-one, to approach folks I didn't know, on their property, with only a smile as an introduction, was an overwhelming idea. At the same time, the prospect of creating strong, meaningful portraits motivated me to confront this challenge. The article for *Mountain Living* gave me both the motivation and rationale I needed to get started. I made trips with friends to visit people they knew in the area, and found it very rewarding. To connect with someone I had never met, and establish a level of trust that would allow me to create a portrait that spoke of that person, was unbelievable, even magical. Reinforced by these positive experiences I began to venture out on my own, roaming the mountains where I grew up. This was something I had been doing for years—an adventure rewarded by unseen landscapes—but now I proceeded with an eye out for people. When I saw someone out working I found it best to simply stop the car, get out, and start walking toward the person. At that point there was no turning back—I had to say something. I soon realized that once the conversation was initiated, listening was much more important than talking, and I only needed to ask a few questions to keep the conversation going. This was not difficult as I was very interested in learning about them and their lives.

I also met people at social events, church gatherings, and in the fields where they worked. They, in turn, guided me in new directions. For instance, while photographing a view of a small cove, I noticed an aging woman on the back porch of a cabin. Stopping by the farm, I found her brother, James Davis, and his wife, Portia, working in their garden. We visited awhile, and I made a photograph of them, as well as one of Alice Davis, the woman I had first noticed, sitting in her chair on the porch. On a subsequent trip, I met the couple's daughter, Peggy Harmon, who told me about a man who made molasses at his farm in another part of the county. That led me to James Hylton and his family, who allowed me to photograph the all-day process of molasses making.

As to why they let me into their lives and agreed to be photographed, I can only speculate. In some ways I think they were flattered (and somewhat baffled) by my genuine interest in them and fascination with the ordinary, everyday events of their lives. But I think that spending time with each person was the most important factor. Although normally private and cautious with strangers, once they were comfortable with my presence, they would relax and share their stories with me. While no one professed to like having their picture made, few refused, although most good-naturedly demurred at first. They were accommodating, patient, and generous with their time. I would always take prints back to them as a way of saying thanks, but regret that many of them are not alive today to see the material in its present book form, and that I could not include all of the people I photographed.

Over the years I have been involved with this, I have seen the continuation of trends already at work in the rural communities. Modern ways supplant many traditions. The mountains don't insulate as well as they once did. Satellite dishes funnel television to even the remotest regions, bringing its culturally homogenizing impact into every home. Uniqueness is disappearing. Many of the younger generation are leaving their parents' farms, choosing not to tend the land as their ancestors had done. As a consequence, the size of the average family farm has shrunk significantly. Consolidation and mechanization have replaced the small independent farmer and his draft animals, and food production is now concentrated into fewer hands. Most of those who remain grow such cash crops as tobacco instead of fruits and vegetables.

Paul Dockery with horses, breaking the ground, 1981 • Anderson Branch, Madison County, NC

The migration to the cities and suburbs has resulted in sprawl. Shopping strips, business parks, and national chain and convenience stores dot the once-rural landscape. The paved roads that formerly brought great promise and opportunity for the farmer now benefit the new commuting residents. Developers are buying farmland, subdividing it, paving it over, and building tract housing projects and gated communities. This has distorted property values, and the small farmer can no longer financially compete for productive land. The land itself has become the commodity rather than the products it once yielded. New homes dot the ridgelines as retirees and summer residents play "king of the mountain," curbed only by road builders' and well diggers' limitations. Long-range views are valued more than fertile bottomland, proximity to a water source, or a sheltering cove. Much of the farmland now sits idle. The historic connection to the land has suffered, and few members of the newer generations feel the spiritual bond that the farmer had with the land in the past. Our new lifestyle has cost us an important link to the natural world that sustains us.

While there is no stopping the transformations that are under way, I believe we can learn from the past and honor the rural inhabitants by preserving some record of their lives for future generations—a way of life that has all but disappeared with the passing of those born in the first few decades of the twentieth century. My hope is that this book offers the reader some insight into the lives of the farmers—their values, the challenges they faced, and how they coped with what life brought them. For me, this project has been an exciting exploration of this remote mountainous region, the people who live there, and my heritage. Learning about their lives has enabled me to better understand my own, and appreciate my place in the community and society at large. I plan to continue roaming the mountains, make new friends, and share their lives through conversation and photography.

TIM BARNWELL

The Face of Appalachia

People and the Land

Collie Payne and steer, Berry, at barn, 1981 • Big Pine Creek, Madison County, NC

Leona Rice quilting, 1980 • Mars Hill, Madison County, NC

Charlie Thomas, 1981 • Walnut, Madison County, NC

Mountain farm view, 1982 • Rector's Corner, Madison County, NC

B. W. Payne on hay rake, 1981 • Little Pine Creek, Madison County, NC

Homer Reeves with family photographs, 1983 • Spring Creek, Madison County, NC

Virgie and Amos Henderson, 1982 • Lonesome Mountain, Madison County, NC

Mabel Cutshall with broom straw, 1983 • Shelton Laurel section, Madison County, NC

Harold Garrison, woodcarver, 1980 • Jupiter, Buncombe County, NC

Mary Jane Queen, 2002 • Caney Fork, Jackson County, NC

Car in creek, 1982 • Madison County, NC

Elmore Helton in garden, 1982 • Walnut section, Madison County, NC

Farm buildings receding up hillside, 1983 • Little Pine Creek, Madison County, NC

Ball City Baptist Church, 1998 • Spring Creek, Madison County, NC

Tobacco

James Griffith with horse in field, 1983 • Pensecola section, Yancey County, NC

James Burnette family with friend setting tobacco, 1984 • California Creek, Madison County, NC

Davis family in tobacco field, 1982 • Brush Creek, Madison County, NC

Ed Plemmons cutting tobacco, 1982 • Dry Branch section, Madison County, NC

Ramsey family in tobacco field, 1985 • Doe Branch section, Madison County, NC

Donald Williams and Chris, 1981 • Spring Creek, Madison County, NC

Seven men on break from cutting tobacco, 1981 • Sodom Laurel section, Madison County, NC

41

William and Pearl Shelton taking tobacco to barn, 1981 • Crooked Ridge Lane, Madison County, NC

Ed Plemmons grading tobacco, 1982 • Dry Branch section, Madison County, NC

43

"Marlboro Men" at Coates Grocery, 1982 • Petersburg, Madison County, NC

Ray Owen, tobacco warehouse owner, 1985 • Asheville, Buncombe County, NC

Business and Handicrafts

Turk Franklin and Delmos Cook at Cook's Service Station, 1981 • Belva section, Madison County, NC

Pink Plemmons store, 1983 • Luck, Madison County, NC

Know Brigman and Dorothy Shupe at Walnut Post Office and General Store, 1982 • Walnut, Madison County, NC

Howard Allen and Jacksie Roberts, junkyard, 1983 • Brush Creek, Madison County, NC

Doby Reed in cycle junkyard, 1983 • Del Rio, Cocke County, TN

Four men at Canton Hardwood sawmill, 2001 • Canton, Haywood County, NC

James "Pop" Story on Linotype machine, 1982 • Marshall, Madison County, NC

Oma Hensley and daughter, Pansy Cutshall, 1981 • Spillcorn, Madison County, NC

Emma Mills with quilts, 1982 • Dry Branch section, Madison County, NC

Marian Anderson, rug hooking, 1980 • Beech Glen, Madison County, NC

Rita Johnson, quilting, 1982 • Big Pine Creek, Madison County, NC

Food Production

Rolling hills and truck, 1988 • Paint Fork, Yancey County, NC

Ola Barnes in garden, 1982 • Sprinkle's Branch Road, Madison County, NC

Donald Williams and Roy Mathis in garden, 1981 • Spring Creek, Madison County, NC

Emma Mills on porch with chickens, 1982 • Dry Branch section, Madison County, NC

Ruby Roberts and mother, Hattie, 1981 • Rector's Corner, Madison County, NC

Fred Barnett, shucking corn, 1980 • Hot Springs, Madison County, NC

Lloyd Fish and dog, Brownie, with wood shingles, 1980 • Spring Creek, Madison County, NC

Kella Buckner and Clyde Massey, working hay, 1981 • Big Pine Creek, Madison County, NC

Clyde Massey and horse, Trigger, 1981 • Big Pine Creek, Madison County, NC

Morning along the creek, 1982 • Roberts Hill Road, Madison County, NC

L. D. "Buck" Fender grinding cane, 1984 • Foster Creek, Big Laurel, Madison County, NC

Buck Fender stirring molasses, 1984 • Foster Creek, Big Laurel, Madison County, NC

Molasses making, Hylton Farm, 1984 • Foster Creek, Big Laurel, Madison County, NC

71

Amos Henderson and Alvin Chandler, 1981 • Lonesome Mountain, Madison County, NC

Rita and Jeff Johnson, canning, 1985 • Big Pine Creek, Madison County, NC

Winter

Toney Plemmons' farm in snow, 1989 • Meadow Fork, Madison County, NC

Farm and valley in snow, 1987 • Grapevine section, Madison County, NC

Two barns in snow, 1989 • Walnut, Madison County, NC

Bear hunting club, Christmas Eve, 1982 • Mill Ridge above Hot Springs, Madison County, NC

Dempsey Woody and hunting dogs, 1983 • Bluff section, Madison County, NC

Rex Meadows and son, Kevin, bear hunting, 1982 • Mill Ridge, Madison County, NC

Bob Roberts and dog, 1982 • Rector's Corner, Madison County, NC

Griffin farm in snow, 1987 • Big Laurel, Madison County, NC

Cabin in snow on ridge, 1985 • Marshall area, Madison County, NC

D. W. Griffith and John Kilpatrick, hog killing, 1983 • Upper Hominy Valley, Buncombe County, NC

McKinley "Doc" Caldwell, 1980 • Big Pine Creek, Madison County, NC

Religion

Ernest Rector, 1983 • Marshall, Madison County, NC

Walnut Methodist Church, cabin, in snow, 1982 • Walnut, Madison County, NC

River baptism, Arrington Branch Baptist Church, 1982 • Grapevine section, Madison County, NC

Leicester church in snow, 1982 • Leicester, Buncombe County, NC

Alma Ferguson and Virginia Teague, at Swann funeral, 1984 • Rector's Corner, Madison County, NC

Walnut Methodist Church cemetery, 1982 • Walnut, Madison County, NC

Alice Davis being comforted by niece, Peggy Harmon, 1983 • Grapevine section, Madison County, NC

Dry Branch Church, 1982 • Dry Branch, Madison County, NC

Girls in church doorway, Arrington Branch Baptist Church, 1983 • Grapevine section, Madison County, NC

Portraits

Byard Ray playing fiddle, 1978 • Asheville, Buncombe County, NC

Kate Church, 1980 • Hot Springs, Madison County, NC

Lewis Roberts, 1981 • Alexander section, Buncombe County, NC

Amanda Gunter on porch, 1983 • Sodom Laurel, Madison County, NC

Zola Payne with husband, Collie, 1981 • Big Pine Creek, Madison County, NC

Homer Reeves and son, Clyde, 1981 • Spring Creek, Madison County, NC

Bertha Marler and daughter, Myrtle, 1983 • Marshall, Madison County, NC

Ernest Teague at Swann farm, 1984 • Rector's Corner, Madison County, NC

Aunt Laura Cook, 1981 • Gahagan farm, Shelton Laurel, Madison County, NC

Lloyd Rigsby, 1979 • Walnut section, Madison County, NC

Bud Norton and horse, Kate, 1982 • Grapevine section, Madison County, NC

Collie Payne and steer, Berry, in tobacco field, 1981 • Big Pine Creek, Madison County, NC

John Chandler and gamecocks, 1984 • Mars Hill, Madison County, NC

Charlie Thomas (right) and friend, Joe, 1981 • Brush Creek, Madison County, NC

Ernie Metcalf, daughter Amy Edgins, and grandson James, 1983 • Big Laurel section, Madison County, NC

Collins family on porch, 1983 • Parrotsville, Cocke County, TN

Wade Massey, 1982 • Big Pine Creek, Madison County, NC

Evia Metcalf, 1981 • Spillcorn, Madison County, NC

Tammy and Amanda Gunter, cousins, 1983 • Shelton Laurel, Madison County, NC

B. W. Payne and family, taking break, 1981 • Little Pine Creek, Madison County, NC

Oral Histories

Following are text passages taken from conversations I had with many of the people I photographed over the years. They are excerpts from stories told about their lives, taken from recordings made either at the time the photograph was created or on a subsequent visit. They are the words of the person shown or, in the case of a landscape image, from someone who spoke about a subject related to the photograph. These recollections represent an oral history and, as such, are only as factually accurate as the memories of the persons involved and may occasionally be tinted by time and forgetfulness. Nevertheless they allow the viewer to see events through the eyes of the subject and provide further context for the photographs.

Portia Davis
page 2

My daddy used to say that poor folks have poor folks ways and rich folks have mean ones. I was raised poor and I've never gotten above a cornbread living. When I was a girl, you were lucky if you had one winter dress and one summer dress, and I never had more than one pair of shoes at a time. I would've liked to have had a little more when I was younger, but I'm old now and it doesn't seem to matter much anymore. We've always made do with what we had and we've always been happy. We've always been able to count on our family and friends to help out when we needed it.

B. W. Payne
page 8

I've lived in Little Pine all my life. I bought this place about twenty-five years ago. We raised five children here, but they all live away from here now. They're still good about coming back to help out though, especially on days like today when there's more work than a man can handle alone.

Farming is hard work for sure, but it's not this much work every day. I had to come to work today just like everybody else, but after the hay is up, I won't have this much to do again for a while.

I use a tractor around the farm some now, but you can't use one this far up on steep land like this. It's just too dangerous. You hear about them turning over on people every year, and most don't live through that. We use horse-drawn equipment up here. It's safer, and it's quiet, too. You really got to know your animals and what they're capable of when you're farming this kind of steep land. You're trusting them with your life.

Amos Henderson
page 10

I raised this chicken like a man would a pet. When he was young he got his foot caught between two pieces of tin. It got pretty messed up and I had to cut it all the way off. I should have killed him then but I didn't. I kept him. Now I take care of him just like a man would a cat or a dog.

At night he climbs the bank and stays in the little house I built for him. He flies down here the next morning and I feed him, because he can't scratch for food like the others. I was thinkin' about cuttin' him a wooden leg out of cedar to help him stand up. I think I could do it, too.

Paul Dockery
page 15

We're breaking new ground for farming. This land hasn't been worked in over fifteen years. It was really grown up. We had to clear it, burn off the brush, and pull up the big rocks and stumps. It's pretty rough going, but up here you learn to use what you've got.

When you're breaking up new ground like this, you run into rocks and roots and all sorts of obstacles that have to be moved or worked around. You're always starting and stopping. These horses have been used for logging of late. They're used to pulling a big load at a hard pace. Once you start 'em they really take off and don't want to stop. Most times it takes two of us just to hold them back.

Collie Payne
page 19

My wife Zola and I have lived on this farm about thirty-two years. I built my house and put up this barn during World War II. Cut timber right off the land to make it. I built my place up here because I like the mountains, I like to hunt, and I like my own privilege. I've hunted all my life and that's one reason I live up here where I do. I've had one pistol for twenty-five years. I killed nine 'coons my first hunt

with it. Now, if I'm working with my steer Berry—
and my fields are about half a mile straight on up
the mountain through the woods—and Zola gets
sick, or someone comes to the house, all she has to
do is come out on the cabin porch and fire it once
and I know she needs me. I can tell its "pop" from
any other in this valley.

Leona Rice
page 20

My grandfather worked for twenty-five cents a day
cradling wheat. If they didn't have the money to pay
him, they would give him a piece of fatback or a
small poke of wheat in return. When I was younger,
I worked nine and a half hours a day and four and a
half on Saturday, and got paid twenty-eight dollars
every two weeks. I also made some extra money
from quilting.

I learned to quilt from my mother and grand-
mother. I started piecing when I was ten and made
my first quilt at seventeen. It took between two and
two-and-a-half weeks to make a queen-size quilt,
working in our spare time. We'd work in the garden
while it was cool, in the morning and afternoon,
and would come in when it got too hot to work outside and do some quilting.

Back then you'd consider it a good living to get
five dollars for one. People made them for covering
and warmth, when you didn't have oil stoves—just
a fireplace to heat the whole house. They almost
disappeared when oil heat came along. Now they're
used more for decoration than anything else, and
they bring hundreds of dollars, depending on the
quality and design.

There are many different styles of quilts. For
instance, a log cabin quilt is made up of lots of
small narrow pieces and takes a longer time to make
than the larger patchwork ones. There's even a couple of dozen color patterns for different log cabin
quilts.

Charlie Thomas
page 21

I used to farm and I enjoyed it, until I got where I
wasn't able any longer. Even when I was growing up
we raised almost everything we ate. You'd buy a little
coffee if you wanted it, but we never drank it, and
buy or trade for what sugar you needed, and we
used honey for that. We've always kept bees for our
own honey. I've been around bees all my life—
about fifty years. I've got nine hives of my own now.
I use a hood over my head when I rob the hives, but
I smoke the bees first to make them calm. I always
get a few stings, but it don't bother me much. We
have honey every year from these hives, and usually
end up with enough extra to give to neighbors. If
you have sourwood trees and such around where
you keep your bees, you get the best tasting honey
there is.

Ernest Teague
page 22

I grew up in that old farmhouse right down there on
the ridge. When I was a boy we moved here from
Marshall. I remember coming across the mountain,
in the snow, on the back of a sled pulled by horses.
That was the first time I saw this land and there

wasn't a cleared place to be found. All that pasture-land stood in trees. There was a big snow on the ground and I remember how cold it was. I was all bundled up on the back of the sled. That was around 1921. I guess I was about four years old. It was the first thing I can remember.

The man my father bought this land from, found a little black boy down by the railroad tracks one day. The little fellow wasn't but about four or five years old, and didn't know who he was or where he came from. This man took him in and raised him like he was one of his own. He named him George Osborne. When he grew up I reckon he cleared more land than any other man in these parts. He loved to work and clear trees. He's buried up at the Rector cemetery with the rest of the family.

It took a lot of years and plenty of hard work to clear that land for pasture and farming. My father cleared a lot of it in the years we lived here. We also had a family of tenant farmers who lived on our land and helped work and clear it. If my father provided them with a team of horses to work with, then he would get half of what they made in a year. If they had their own team, he got a third instead. We only had one tenant family at a time on our farm.

I remember one tenant farmer from Greenville, South Carolina, who lived with us for about five years. He had four or five children and they all lived in a small log house up the hollow. Folks had big families back then. The more kids you had, the more land you could tend. This family had dogs and chickens, and raised their own corn and wheat for bread, and tended a garden. I don't see how folks made it, especially after they had to split what little they made with the landowner. It was hard on everyone.

Folks didn't have fertilizers and such back then, so they had to clear two or three acres, or whatever they could, beginning in the fall, so they'd have

"new" ground to plant their crops on each year. To clear the land, they'd start by "grubbing" the trees, which means they cut the brush out and the bottom limbs up three or four feet or so, and then take big crosscut saws into the stand and fall the trees. They'd cut the remaining limbs off and then roll the logs down each side of the hill into the hollows. I've seen them burn stacks of logs, virgin timber it was, that were forty or fifty feet high. Today, of course, they'd use it to make lumber, or at least for firewood, but back then all they had *was* wood.

B. W. Payne
page 23

Years ago there were two schoolhouses along this one creek, and a mill right down there along the bottom. The Presbyterians used to treat this area as a mission field, building hospitals and schools and such. They even ran a private school in the big white house across the road there. Now kids have to take a bus off to school somewhere.

These hills used to be full of people. There was a farm or two up every hollow. Throughout the Depression years, folks couldn't find jobs nowhere anyway, so they had to stay on the farms to make a living. When World War II came, it created a lot of jobs and things really began to change. People began to travel and move outside the area for work. Now there are not many of us left.

Homer Reeves
page 24

Virgie Henderson
page 25

When your wife dies its awful hard. The best part of me is gone. She was born October 24, 1895, and was buried on her eighty-sixth birthday. We were married for sixty-three years.

We were both twenty-three when we got married. If a man doesn't know what he wants by that time, there's somethin' the matter with him. We didn't exactly get along all the time you know, but we never had any what you might call serious disagreements.

After my wife and I were engaged I was gone twice for over a year. One time was after the big flood, to fix power lines from Atlanta to Birmingham, Alabama, for the company I worked for. They paid me six dollars and twenty-five cents a week for ten hours a day back then. The other time was to Europe, in the army during World War I. She waited for me to get back from France after the war. We didn't waste much time gettin' married once I got back. We didn't have much to speak of at the time. She was a schoolteacher and all I had was the clothes on my back and the little poke they gave me when I got out of the service.

I still miss her terribly every day, but I'm thankful for the family I've got left. I have eleven grandchildren and seven great grandchildren now, and they really pitch in to look after me.

Amos has been helping me get some clothes washed and out on the line today. I'm afraid it's gonna snow tonight and we need some clean clothes. I haven't been able to work much of late. Not feeling all that well. As it is, I have to bundle up just to hang the clothes out. You can't take that many chances when you're eighty-two! Amos has been a great help though.

I've lived all my life on this Lonesome Mountain. Raised eight children here, too—three by my first husband, and five more with Amos. I married Amos in 1927. I had three boys at the time. Joe was six, Glen was about four, and my youngest was Claude. He lacked six days of being three months old when his father died. That was 1923. His father was a brakeman on the railroad, and was killed when he fell down between two railroad cars.

I hung with my boys all their life. I've never been away from 'em for a week. I hung right with 'em until the army took 'em. The children all treat Amos like they didn't know no other father, and he treats 'em all like they was his own. I couldn't have done no better than Amos. All our children are gone from here but two, and they call ever day or so to check on us. It's hard to get 'em all back together. We got the whole family together last summer for a reunion and now we've got over twenty grandchildren and about half that many great-grandchildren.

I'm not looking forward to winter. We have hard winters on this mountain. It's time to get up wood now, but Amos split his thumb open down to the bone cuttin' wood the other day. Now he's not able to do any more. There's another fellow who's supposed to come and help us as soon as he gets his tobacco up. I don't know what we'd do if we didn't have friends or family to help us out.

Mabel Cutshall
page 27

I've made my own brooms for as long as I can remember. I don't like the store-bought kind. They don't last very long and don't work as well as the ones you make yourself. My son "Glady" got me some long "broom corn" and I made this one myself. All you have to do is get you a stick for a handle and fasten the stalks to it with some string or wire. You boil some water and pour it over the stalks to make them softer and then fasten 'em real tight to the stick with string or wire. The long kind works the best 'cause you can fasten more of it to the stick.

I had eight children, some of 'em are dead now. I had one who only lived seven days. It was all blue around the head and throat and had the death rattles. Glady lives with me now and I'm glad of that. He watches after me but I don't take no money from him. He broke both his legs helpin' somebody else work their tobacco a while back, but still does most of the plantin' and such around here. I do a lot of chores myself still. I feed the chickens and bring in some kindlin' for the fire. I used to milk the cows but my arms aren't strong enough anymore. I can only get a trickle out of 'em now, so Glady does the milkin'.

Harold Garrison
page 28

A few years ago people had a way of doing things and then the "modern ways" came along and the older jobs seemed like torture in comparison. They figured the sooner they were rid of them the better. Now people are a wanting the old ways back and it's almost too late—they're about gone. People don't remember how to do things for themselves anymore, or they never learned how, and the ones who do are getting old and dying out. Very few could even raise a garden to feed themselves today, much less run a farm. I grew up during the Depression years and what you didn't grow, you didn't have.

Lots of skills, like quilt making and canning food and making things with your hands, are disappearing. I've made wooden toys to sell for about ten years now. Mostly things like wooden flowers, dancing dolls, carved animals and such. I travel around to some of the local fairs and sell what I make, but I always like coming back home. These mountains around here are cozy. Lots of hills, hollows, and coves. You go out west where they're really big, and they make you stand back and look. They're not with you. Around here well, I guess you could say they become a part of you.

Mary Jane Queen
page 29

I sing the old time ballads. A lot of people don't understand but a ballad tells a story, either a murder story or a love story, and lots of time they're both combined together. But if you put music to a ballad

you've got to speed it up and it's not a ballad then. You've got to get it with your music or it don't sound right, or you've got to slow your music down enough and that ruins the tune, so that's the reason the ballad is sung without any accompaniment.

I have eight children—four boys and four girls. Ever one of 'em plays music but the two oldest girls. Everybody's got their own style of playin'—some like one thing and some like another. Lots of my family plays bluegrass and lots plays the country music, but we all likes and loves the old mountain songs—like my dad and all of them played back then.

My dad used to sing all the time. He was a banjo player, too. Any kind of entertainment they had around through this area, they always called him to go and play. He really knew the songs. Uncle Albert Brown had a big barn over on Caney Fork where they had barn dances. Dad played the banjo and Glen Wilson played the fiddle—that's all the instruments they used to have, you know. All the young people went. I always loved to hear him play—so I guess maybe that's why I turned out to be a banjo player, too.

Elmore Helton
page 31

I worked in Swannanoa at a lumber mill for almost seventeen years. We got a ten-minute break in the morning and ten minutes in the afternoon. They would let us take home any broken lumber they had. Times was hard back then, too, so while everyone else was takin' their break and foolin' around, I'd be out there cuttin' up wood to take home to burn in the cook stove and fireplace.

Folks in these mountains have always had to scrape together to make it by. Back during the

Depression, there weren't no jobs, so you were lucky if you had a piece of land to grow some food on. When the Second World War was on, everyone had to pitch in for the war effort. Every piece of old scrap, any piece of metal lying around—it was all valuable. They needed it. We'd gather up whatever we could spare and take it to the collections for the war. I guess I learned to keep a lot of what most folks would consider junk, but when times are hard you never know what might come in handy.

Norman Baker
page 32

When I was a boy of ten or twelve, about the age of my twin sons now, I remember the hillside across from my house looking like a snowstorm had hit, it was so white with the trunks of dead chestnut trees. The bark had peeled off of them and was bleached white.

Men came in and set up a sawmill on the farm. They cut down the trees—some as big around as a pickup truck hood—and drug them down to where the steam boilers were set up. The boilers were hooked up to a big old seventy-two-inch saw blade and were fired off of slats and sawdust. It would get so hot you couldn't stand near them. I remember watching the sparks and pieces of burning wood leap out of the chimney of the mill and disappear into the sky. It was quite a sight. I was only a lad, but I remember it to this day.

They would cut the trees into planks and haul them down to the main road by horse and wagon, then out on trucks from there. There's still a lot of original mountain chestnuts today, but they're all small. They only get to be about six or seven years old before the blight hits them. There's not many big trees left of any kind any more. They've all been cut down, shipped out, and sawed up for lumber.

Plato Worley
page 33

I remember one time when my brother was plowing with a mule and I was still young enough to ride the beam, which was the post that ran back from mule to plow. I would sit on it and the mule would pull and my brother would guide it. My brother was behind the mule one day and it kicked him and split his face wide open from the side of his nose down to his lip. It busted out a couple of teeth and my brother passed out right there in the field. I ran to the house and got my father. He carried my brother up to the front porch and laid him down. He went in the house and got some corn liquor and silk thread. He poured the wound full of liquor and then sewed him up while he was lying there. He did a good job, too, 'cause when they took the stitches out, it barely even left a scar.

People didn't used to go to the doctor much. They were either too far away or couldn't afford one, so they learned to doctor themselves. My father lost his arm in an accident and never went to see a

doctor, and he did fine. It happened before I was born. When he was in his early twenties he was working in a grinding mill. His sleeve got caught in the corkscrew of the water-driven wheel and as it turned it twisted his arm right out of its socket. He passed out of course, but they carried him up to the house and poured corn liquor into his shoulder to clean it out. Corn liquor was strong stuff back then. They put homemade poultices on the wound and for weeks after that my mother could remember drawing sawdust out of his shoulder. He never went to the doctor or nothing and lived to father nine children.

Somehow they stopped the bleeding. I don't know how, they may have read the scripture to him to make it stop. There's a verse in the Bible that you can use to stop people from bleeding. It's Ezekiel, Chapter 16, starting from the fourth verse down. The sixth verse is the main one. If someone is bleeding bad and you can't get it stopped, you can call out their name and then read the scripture over them and the bleeding will stop. I've seen it work on many a person and on other things, too, including mules and horses. There's been a lot of people's lives saved that way before fancy doctors and hospitals came along. God gave Christians tools like that to help them survive all these centuries.

James Griffith
page 35

I like plowing with a horse. It's a lot harder work than using a tractor, but you can work slower, make tighter turns, and keep from damaging your crops. Once you work a horse and you get to know each other, they can tell what you want usually before you tell them. You get to know each other's pace, and it makes the job a lot easier on both of you. She and I have worked together for so long I barely even have to pull on the reins to get her to turn, or slow down, or do whatever I want.

I like using a hand plow and harness to weed tobacco. After it gets up a bit, everything else in the soil wants to grow with it, so you have to till the soil between the tobacco plants to uproot the weeds. This is a fair-size field but it don't take too long to till it over, once you get harnessed up.

I've worked on this farm for a lot of years, and we've always done things this way. You see a lot of other places around changing, but I like the old ways. You really get to know the piece of land you're working, 'cause you're walking it every day, your feet right down in the soil, instead of riding around with a motor going all the time. I don't like the noise nor the smell of a tractor. I like working with a horse and the feel of the reins in my hands.

Anita Davis
page 37

I'm originally from Michigan, but my husband grew up here. We were living up there until about five years ago. We had a nice brick house with a two-car garage in the suburbs, but we were bored with our life. When you work in a factory or some big operation, you don't feel like you make much of a difference, you have such a small part in what they're making. There was nothing much to do except go off to work and come home and watch television.

We really didn't spend much time with each other and didn't want to raise our kids that way. We longed for this type of life, so we moved back here and started farming the way we did growing up. It's a hard life but we like it a lot. When you work together as a family to make something, it makes you closer to each other—you share the hard times as well as the good.

Ed Plemmons
page 38

My grandfather told me how tell when your tobacco is ready to harvest. He said to cut a stalk and look at the wood in it. If it looks like cornbread that's been cooked with too much baking soda—kinda yellow you know—that's when it's ready.

Once you figure out it's ready, you cut it at the base of the stalk and strip off the leaves. You push the leaves down over a wooden stake and let them dry out in the field a few days. Then you carry it out to the barn and hang it up and let it dry out real good for a couple of months. Before you take it to market you grade it out into stacks by how good it is.

They have auctions at the tobacco warehouses in Asheville and Greenville. Buyers from all the big tobacco companies come. They walk through and bid on it. If it's a good year you might make out okay, but it's a poor living at best. I share my crop with the landlord. He owns the land and the machinery—I grow the tobacco and tend it.

Mr. and Mrs. Ramsey
page 39

Today we're working a small patch of tobacco. We have an allotment we can grow every year, and it helps bring in some cash money, which really helps out when you've got children to provide for. Mindy is eleven and Lela is six. They ride the school bus home, and then change clothes to help us around the farm. Lela especially can't wait to get home and change out of her dress and get old clothes on that she can get dirty. They're both a big help though.

Donald Williams
page 40

When everybody else is working tobacco I take care of the ones younger than me. We play hide-and-seek in the tobacco, or around the barn, while our parents are working the fields. When I get older, I'll get to help with the crops, and somebody else will watch the younger kids.

Dwight Roberts
page 41

When there's work to be done, like cutting tobacco, we all chip in and help each other out. We'll work one person's field at a time till we get them all done. It's a lot easier that way, and better for everyone concerned. The work seems to go faster, and it's nice to have the company of friends helping out. Seems like country people have always done things that way.

William and Pearl Shelton
page 42

I've worked tobacco all my life, except for seven years during the Second World War. When I was a boy we worked flue-cured tobacco like they do down in the eastern part of the state now. You'd have to dry it in big barns. They were log back then—they didn't have plank barns. You'd have to make them airtight, so you'd fill in the gaps between the logs with "chinks". These were strips of wood four or five feet long that you'd wedge in the cracks from the outside. Then you'd find a clay spot of ground and mix you up some mud and clay and go on the inside of the barn and fill in the remaining cracks. Next you'd build furnaces, usually two, out of stone. You'd run some twelve-inch pipe from them around the bottom of the barn, and then vent them up the side and out. Your tobacco would be hanging in there and you'd build up your wood fires in your furnaces until the heat got up to about 190 degrees. It had to stay at least that hot day and night until it was cured like you wanted it. If the temperature dropped below that, the sap would run back down into the leaves and streak them.

You didn't pull the leaves off the stalks then like they do down east now. Back then you just staked it and hung it the barns like we do burley tobacco now. Once you got the yellow that you wanted on the leaves, you raised the temperature from 190 degrees to about 285 degrees and left it there till it cured out. That usually took about seven days. Now the people working flue-cured use portable sheds and oil heat to cure with, and it only takes a couple of days I think.

I remember the big thermometers we had hung in the barns. Somebody would have to stay at the barn and keep the fires built up so the temperature wouldn't drop. When the parents would go back up to the house, us children would stay at the barn, 'cause somebody had to watch the temperature all the time. We'd take turns locking each other in the barn and see who could stay in the longest. It's a wonder we didn't suffocate and die in there as hot and closed up as it was.

We work burley tobacco now. Our children came down to help us put this crop up. This year we got a dollar and eighty-five cents a pound for our tobacco. We got ten thousand just out of this piece of bottomland. We separated and graded it and took it to market on seven-hundred-pound baskets. You bale it up instead of pulling the leaves off, and sell it like that. People don't do that much anymore, but that's one reason we got a better price than most.

Johnny Coates
page 44

I ran a store up on Grapevine for a good while, but it's been closed twenty-five or thirty years now. A lot of people still come by and look at it. Awhile back a girl came by and wanted to buy some old signs off it. I sold her some paper ones from the inside and some metal ones off the outside. I couldn't figure why she wanted them, but she sure was happy to get 'em.

We've got about fourteen or fifteen hundred pounds of tobacco this year, between my son's fields and mine. It should bring a good price—upwards around a dollar and eighty-one cents a pound. They just passed a new tax on each pack of cigarettes that will probably make lots of smokers give it up.

I had to give up smoking the hard way though. I slipped and fell a couple of winters back, on the road below my house. I was on the way down to get my tractor. I landed on a rock and busted my ribs. One of them punctured my lung. I lay there for a good while, and then tried hard to crawl back up to the house to let my wife know I was hurt. A girl that lived about a mile up the road happened by and she and my wife got me back to the house. They took me to the hospital and I had to stay there eighteen days. They kept me under oxygen most of the time. Now I have to take it a bit easier.

Delmos Cook
page 47

My uncle moved into this store in 1928, I believe it was. A few years later another fellow and I went in partners on it for about seven years, then I got out of it for a while. A little later I moved back in, and now I've got thirty-eight years in this store. That's a lifetime, really.

There's not many stores like this left now. Used to be there were several up every creek. There was a fellow named Major Tweed that used to run a store and post office up at Whiterock, near the old hospital. Even back then a lot of stores had closed up and he explained it the best I've heard it. He told me that there's not a merchant around but what's pullin' for better roads for the community, and cuttin' his own throat all the while. See, when the better roads came in, people could travel farther, and didn't do as much business around where they lived. They didn't need stores as close to home once they could get out more. Now we mostly just sell gas, soft drinks, and cigarettes.

Amos Henderson
page 48

I like to pay for what I can. Ever once in a while a man needs credit. There's not a store in this county that I couldn't go to and get what I wanted today,

and pay for it when I could. As long as I tell a man when I'll pay him, and keep my word, I got good credit.

I can go to town in Marshall and get two, three, four hundred dollars worth of stuff I need, and pay the man when I get my tobacco in, or pay him a little along as I can each month. If I ever couldn't pay, I'd just go to the man and tell him before it was due, and work it out with him. As long as you do that—be honest with the fellow and tell him what you're gonna do, and keep your word—you'll be treated right.

Knox Brigman
page 49

This post office here has been in the store about nineteen years. My wife operated it till she passed away about four years ago. It's not a Class A post office, it's a Class C. That's what they call a rural post office. It's not run by the civil service, it's contracted out. You bid on it every so often to keep it. There used to be four or five post offices like this one just up Big Pine Creek alone, but now it's the only one like it still left in Madison County. Today I don't even have a Walnut stamp anymore. They pick up the mail and take it to Asheville every day and bring it back stamped.

This post office here in Walnut is to serve the local people. We have about 25 boxes rented and serve about 350 general delivery customers at the window. Dorothy Shupe has had Box 44 as long as the post office has been here, and I think that was her number when it was in the old store, too. She may have had the same box forty years now.

Rural carriers have taken over from these type operations though. Back years ago there were post offices up every creek, and more than one up some. You traveled from one to the next on horseback though. It was hard to get back into these parts. When the roads got better, they delivered the mail by horse and buggy to each box along the way. Now they use small four-wheel-drive trucks.

Howard Allen
page 50

It seems like every event you go to anymore gets spoiled by a bunch of drunks—the car races, the rodeo that comes to Marshall—it always turns out the same. A group of drunks turn up and spoil the good times for everybody. I've got no use for people who stay drunk all the time. All they want to do is lay around; or it makes 'em mean and they want to fight. It's usually the innocent folks that end up getting hurt, too. One fellow was killed at a bar down on the county line the other night. He heard shootin' and went outside to see what was going on and a stray bullet hit him in the head.

I never drank a can of beer in my life. That's one thing I can say, I've never been drunk. I don't like goin' to things where I know there's goin' to be trouble. I didn't worry about it a bit when I was growin' up, but I don't have the patience for it now. I try to choose better. I went to a Fourth of July picnic over here last week and there was over three hundred people there. Folks were drinkin' some I know, but everyone was havin' a good time and nobody was gettin' out of line or causin' trouble for everyone else. Now that's the way its supposed to be.

Bob Singleton
page 52

I was raised around a sawmill. I grew up over in what's called Dutch Cove. My daddy was a saw man, too. I came to work over here at Canton Hardwood back in 1993. I stayed here awhile, then they needed a loader man up at Winfield Lumber, so they shipped me up there for four or five years till he sold out, and I came back over here.

This is a fair-size sawmill. They can take things pretty much from start to finish. The logs come into the yard on trucks. We unload 'em, then they're scaled and sorted by type of wood—red oak, white oak, pine, poplar, maple, cherry, walnut, whatever. Each one goes in a separate pile till it's ready to be cut. Then they're brought down to the log deck, and a chain pulls them to the debarker, right behind us here. That takes the bark off and gets rid of any dirt and rocks that could ruin a saw. Another chain takes the logs into the buildin' to the band saw. They get cut into ten-by-ten or twelve-by-twelve-inch squares, go through the edger, the resaw, maybe back to the edger, and to the trim saw, where the lumber gets cut to length. It goes on a conveyer out the back of the buildin' to the green line, where guys pull it off and sort it by length onto pallets. Then it's dipped, banded, and taken to the yard where it's regraded, stacked, and stored 'til it's shipped out.

I mainly drive a truck here; haul chips, bark, sawdust. We're able to use all the wood for somethin'. I get rid of everything that's not lumber. I haul shavings and chips down to Champion Paper. They burn the shavings, and use the chips to make paper.

If you work at a place for a long spell like we all have, you get to be friends. Everybody has a job to do and we count on each other to keep things runnin' smooth and to keep an eye out for each other, so nobody gets hurt.

James "Pop" Story
page 53

My father owned a newspaper in the eastern part of the state and bought the *Marshall News-Record* paper in 1924. He ran both for a while, but decided it was too much to handle, so he sold the other one and moved us up here to Marshall. I helped him with the paper from the time I was a boy until he got too old to run it, and then I took it over.

I never really had much help with it. I'd write the news, sell the ads and lay them out, take the pictures with my Polaroid camera, and run the paper over to Waynesville to be printed. I'd wait on it till all hours of the morning, and then come back across the mountain to Marshall, put the addresses on them, take them over to the post office, and mail them before I could go home. I did that every week till I retired in 1970. A fellow came to me and told me he was going to buy me out. I didn't let on that I wanted to sell anyway, but I'd spent thirty-five years meeting deadlines, and to tell you the truth, I was glad to be rid of it. Small town papers, like this one, ran into trouble a few years ago when people started using offset presses. Papers like ours, with a staff of only one or two, couldn't afford to buy them. Some of the bigger newspaper companies started printing the smaller papers on the side, and then they would buy them out.

I like being retired. I do a little commercial printing still on my old German made Mergenthaler Linotype machine here, and I still write a column for the paper once a week. I play checkers a lot more now, too. Checkers is a dying game you might say. Not many take the time to play it anymore. Things are moving too fast today I guess. There's three of us who still play here a lot. I keep a table set up. On Tuesdays we go over to Judson's house for the day to play, and to the senior citizens center in Asheville once a week.

All my friends are still here though. All the folks I got to know so well over the years. They still stop by say "hello" or to chat for a while. That's another nice thing about being retired. You're never too busy to stop and visit with your friends.

Emma Mills
page 55

I learned to quilt from my mother, and she from hers. She could sew anything she sat her mind to. She could make a man's shirt and it would look like it was store bought.

I don't get out from this place much, so when folks is coming by I ask them to bring me some bits and pieces of material so I can keep making quilts. I use whatever material I can get, and try to make the best quilt I can with it. Most of the time I work on them inside, but if it's a real pretty day I'll come out on the porch and work. It's what I do and what I enjoy.

Not many girls are interested in learning to sew anymore. I don't know what to think of young folks today. It seems they don't have a bit of interest in what we have to tell. Got no use for it. Only a few of 'em want to cook or learn to do things around the house. Seems like things went on about the same for generations on end. Now it's all changing so fast, and all the changes have happened in my lifetime it seems. I get confused by it all.

Marian Anderson
page 56

All we have is what we can make. People from outside this area don't realize that we can make so many things with our hands, but we make everything we need—clothes, bonnets, quilts, rugs. We've had to do it all our lives. All the crafts you see in the shops around today grew out of making things you needed around the house, but couldn't afford.

I still make hooked rugs. I learned to make these when I was a young girl. The yarn came from sock tops—waste from the hosiery mills. A lot of folks would get them and dye them to make the colors they wanted. A piece of burlap was used for the backing, and it came from old coffee bean sacks. Back in the twenties and thirties there was a whole industry in these parts making rugs and such. Families all over these mountains made them in their homes to earn extra money. It was a booming business up until World War II. It began to die out when they started bringing them in from Japan and other countries, where they could make them cheaper.

To make a rug like I'm working on here, I start by stretching burlap across a wooden frame. Then I place a paper pattern on top of it and punch holes in the pattern. I make up a mixture of chimney soot and kerosene and paint it over the pattern. When the paper is removed it leaves the design on the burlap. Next I put rug yarn into the burlap with a small, homemade "rug machine" like this one. My husband made it out of a piece of walnut, and old saw, and metal from the gas cap of an old car. It's my favorite and works better than any store-bought one I've seen. When I finish sewing the yarn along the pattern, I've got a finished rug.

I can make two small rugs in a day if I work at it. When I was a girl you could sell a three-foot rug for a $1.00 to $1.50, and you could make two or three a day sometimes. That was good money back then.

Rita Johnson
page 57

This quilt is a wedding present for our friends. Everyone in the community made a separate piece for the quilt top. Now we're sewing the pieces to the backing. We've got one day to finish it up before they get back home, so we've been working a lot of hours this week to get it ready. We want to surprise them with it.

Bud Norton
page 59

I got my first car back in 1927. I've had about five new ones since then. A man could really spend a lot of money on those things if he's not careful. I remember when there wasn't a car in these parts. There wasn't a single paved road in Asheville either at that time, except for one fellow who had a cement walk up to his house. A rich fellow, I guess. That was the only road that wasn't dirt. We used to

haul everything in wagons. Even then you couldn't get a wagon on up in here. You had to bring things in and out on a wooden sled and take them down to the store and load them onto wagons.

We'd haul out tanbark and lumber to Marshall. My father would buy boundaries and we'd go in and cut down trees as big around as a furnace—as big as they come. We'd cut them down up on the mountain, strip the bark off in big lengths, haul it out, and leave the lumber to rot. The bark was worth more than the lumber was. We got twenty dollars a cord for tanbark.

After they got cars in here we'd haul tobacco, chickens, wood, apples, or whatever we had down to the store and load it on the trucks and take it to Marshall. There they'd load it onto trains to send it out to wherever they wanted. Before we had cars, you got around the best way you could—that was either on foot walkin' or on horseback. I remember many a time as a boy I'd go over to Tennessee. It was a two-day ride on horseback.

When I was young, before I was married, when I was runnin' around with a bunch of other fellows, we used to go around playin' music—you know, banjo, fiddle, guitar, whatever we had. We'd just go around to people's houses and play music just to pass the time. We'd ride horseback from place to place all night long, playin' a while at each spot. I remember many a time ridin' through the snow and cold. One time it was so cold and I didn't notice that my feet had frozen in the stirrups, and when I went to get down, I fell off head first into a big snow bank!

Ola Barnes
page 60

I plant my garden by the signs, if you know what that means. I go by the *Farmer's Almanac*. It seems to work, too. This year though I've had to plant three times due to bad weather and the late frost.

My husband used to have this scarecrow in his flower garden. When he died, I put a cover on it and bought it up here. Now it's a female scarecrow. It fools people. I've had them drive by and see her standing up here in the field and tell somebody else that they saw me out working in my garden, and I wasn't even out that day.

Most people make male scarecrows, but I decided to make mine female. It doesn't seem to make any difference to the crows, though. They still come in! I've strung up these pie pans and done everything in the world to keep them out of my garden. Nothing seems to work though, they get used to whatever you do and come on in anyway.

Ruby Roberts
page 63

When I was young I used to love to dance. By the time I was six or seven, I could do the Charleston. Most of what I learned, though, was popular tradi-

tional dances. I would travel around to all the mountain festivals, and I won a lot of awards, and they would make pictures of me. Now I'm older and can't dance no more.

When you get old there's a lot of things you can't do no more. Momma was ninety-five last Sunday. She's been sick lately and can't get around too good, but she still wants to do things. Sometimes she wants to do something so bad, and she can't, that she just sits and cries.

My father was a railroad man. Back when I was little the tracks were marked off in milepost and the engineers would run stretches instead of long hauls. My daddy would drive his train down to a certain milepost, and meet another engineer, and that fellow would take the cars on from there. Then daddy would head back the other direction, and meet another fellow, and get his next load. We lived down the river at Redmond. The railroad ran past there and my daddy could see the house when he went by on his runs.

I was a sickly child and the people that lived next to us had lost their baby to illness. Lots of kids died young like that back then. My daddy always worried after me, so he had momma put a lamp in the front window if everything was all right. He told her to put two lamps in the window if I took sick or died. He would watch for the lamp in our window when he went by the house at night on his run. He told me later how happy he was never to have seen that second light, and how much it comforted him to know things was all well while he was away working.

Fred Barnett
page 64

We've been pretty lucky to make the living we have. My daddy didn't have a penny to leave me when he died. Most families didn't have any more than we did. They were all tenant farmers like us. Tenant farming was a slow way to go. You worked all day and only got half of the wood you had cut, or the crops you had grown, and the landowner got the other half. I remember just after I was married that I worked all day for ten cents an hour to buy a cow for thirty dollars from the landowner. It took me a month of solid work to get up the money.

As I got older I could save a bit, and my wife and I paid a man four hundred dollars to build our first general store, back in 1947. She ran it while I farmed. On in the early sixties we were able to build a small cinder block store in front of the old wooden one. When we first started we had no idea how it would turn out—if we could make a go of it or not. Now we've got years in it, and lots of children and grandchildren to help run it.

When you look back on your life it all seems to make sense—like it couldn't of happened any other way. When you're young you're too busy just putting one foot in front of the other, trying to make your way, raise a family, trying to keep a step ahead, to wonder how it will all turn out. There's no way to tell anyhow—you just got to live it out and do the best you can by others. But I've learned there's an end to all things, and at my age you can see the end of the road—that big shade tree where you're going. When you're young you never even think like that.

Lloyd Fish
page 65

My grandfather made wooden shingles for cabins and churches and such, and he taught my father the trade. My father picked me out of six boys in the family to learn it. I used to make them out of chestnut and mountain oak, but almost all of the chestnut is gone now. Even the new trees, once they get big enough to put out chestnuts, still get the blight. I mostly make wooden shingles now just to show people how it's done.

I tell folks that they should cut shingles and nail them on the house or barn on the old moon and

they will lay flat. If you make them, or nail them on, at the new moon, they're more likely to curl. Lots of folks don't pay attention to the signs anymore, but it's the way I was raised. We always planted our crops by the signs and the almanac, and I've seen plenty of things that make me believe it's true.

Kella Buckner and Clyde Massey
page 66

If you've got mountain land like ours you just about have to work it with horse or mule-drawn equipment. There just ain't no other way. You take small farmers like us; we can't afford thirty or forty thousand dollars for tractors, bailers, and such. If a man had that kind of money, he'd be better off putting it in bonds and such that pay fifteen and sixteen cents on the dollar. With a little, steep farm like this, it wouldn't pay and it'd be too dangerous anyway. As it is, we share what equipment we have, and help out on each other's farms when there's work to be done. A man really depends on his friends and neighbors in these parts.

Clyde Massey
page 67

When I was younger, during the teens and twenties, you were doing good to get a dollar a day farming. That was for ten or more hours a day. My wife worked many a day for twenty cents a day pullin' corn. During the Depression I was in Michigan. I stayed there from the time I was twenty till I was twenty-eight, then I got laid off where I was working and came back here and never went back.

I started buying my farm when I was in my late twenties but didn't move into it until some years later. I've got fifty acres that runs back up behind the house to the top of the hill and across the creek to the top of that hill. My brother lives on the same land, right next to me.

The head of this creek used to be full of people. There were lots of children back then. Now when they get up to eighteen or nineteen years old they leave here and don't come back. They take jobs off somewhere. There's not much in the way of regular jobs in the county to keep them here, unless they farm—and most of them don't want to do that. Now they send two buses up here and there's just a few kids on each of them. One bus comes for the young kids and the other for the high school age.

My horse Trigger was twenty years old this last June. He was born from a mare right here on my farm. I've worked him all that time for corn and tobacco. For what little plowing I need to do he works out better than having a tractor. You really don't need both, and for the type of rough, steep land we have here, a tractor won't do. It'll turn over on you in a minute. People get killed every year like that. It's just too dangerous to use machinery. A horse or a mule still works out best.

Horses live a lot longer now than they used to. When you worked them hard day in and day out for logging and such, by the time they got ten or twelve years old they'd stiffen up so bad you couldn't use them anymore. Now people don't use them for as much, so they live a lot longer.

Folks used to work all their animals more before machinery came along. I've heard about a man who had an old mule. He worked it all its life in this one field he had. The mule must have gone out of its mind one day, 'cause the man found him walking back and forth from one end of that field to another by himself. He did that about twenty times and then just fell over dead. It was just like it was plowing on its own, walking back and forth, back and forth.

Dorothy Rigsby
page 68

I remember once, when my husband Lloyd used to grow wheat, he and some fellows were cradling it in the field above the house. I didn't know if they were going to stay to supper or not, and by the time I found out they were, I had to run down to the store for some things. I never learned to drive, and they didn't build stores on every corner like they do today, so I was about worn out by the time I got back home. Then I had to kill a chicken to fix!

Now, Lloyd had been killing the chickens up to then, so I knew I'd have to learn quick. When he came home he asked how I did it. I had to tell him I'd chased it all over the yard and cut off a leg and one wing before I could get a hold of it good enough to cut off its head like he'd do. It was such a mess, and I felt so sorry for that chicken, even though I knew I was going to kill it anyhow. I got everything done in time though and nobody was the wiser, but I had a young girls legs then. I sure couldn't do it today.

James Hylton
page 69

James Hylton
page 70

Making molasses is a big job. Every fall we go to the fields and cut down the sugar cane. Then we bring it to where we have the mill set up and it's still an all day job. First you have to grind the cane stalks to get the juice. We use a horse to turn the grinder and you have to feed the cane into it as he goes around. The juice runs out and is strained through burlap. You catch it in a bucket, and then cook it all day over the fire until you render it down to molasses, stirring it constantly. Then you pour it off into jars. The kids get to have what's left!

We use a horse to grind the cane. We could use a motor I guess, but I prefer a horse. It's just an old custom I stick with. If you keep on adding motors to everything, we're going to get away from the way things was done once, and the generation below us is not going to know a thing about how it was.

The mill we're using belongs to Buck Fender, and it was his father's before him. Passed down probably by his grandfather. They took the mill from house to house, depending on who needed to use it. It passed through the community that way. Buck says the pole that hooks to the horse is the same one they used when he was a boy. He's sixty-five now, so it's at least that old. I'd guess the mill itself is close to two hundred years old.

People used to depend on molasses mills a lot. You couldn't just run out to the grocery store and buy some. If you didn't make any in the fall, you wouldn't have any for a year. People used it to sweeten about everything when sugar was expensive and hard to come by. I've made molasses all my life, and my father did it before me. We've always had a little patch somewhere—maybe not every year, but I've known it since I was small.

It takes us about fifty-five gallons of juice to make seven or eight gallons of molasses. That boils down to about eight to one. It takes at least three or four hours of constant boiling to make your molasses. We boil ours a little slower than most people. You can do it faster, but you boil a lot of skim into it, and it doesn't have the same taste. You have to stir it the whole time, and keep skimming the green stuff off. It doesn't take that much wood really. Little wood makes better than big. It takes a blaze more than a bed of coals.

I judge when mine's ready by the way it drips off the skimmer; other folks use a thermometer. I go by the old way—when it drips off in about an inch-long drop, and then it's ready. We used to make apple butter in the molasses when I was a boy. Our last run of molasses would be a small one, and we'd core our apples and use the peel and all. Right before the molasses were ready we'd dump our apples in and stir them around. We'd put in spices like cinnamon, but we didn't add sugar. The molasses did the sweetening.

Not many folks make molasses anymore. This is the only spot in the whole Laurel section where it was made this year. People just don't seem to have the time for this type of thing anymore—workin' on jobs away from the farm and all. It's hard work, but more than that, it's confining. When you put a run of molasses on, you can't leave it for a minute until it's done.

James Hylton
page 71

We had three-tenths of an acre of sugar cane planted this year and we made thirty-two gallons. That's approximately ten gallons per tenth acre. We plant around the 15th of May. You can put it in earlier but we plant later so it'll come in after the tobacco, so we don't have to work them both at the same time. It doesn't really take much effort to grow cane. You fertilize and then drop in the seeds. You drop it by guess, then thin it down when the stalks sprout. Then you hoe and plow it like you would corn or anything else, and just watch it. When the seedpod in the head starts to turn from green to red, and it gets a stripe down the stalk, it's ready.

The way most people harvest it is to strip the fodder, and cut the head off, in the field. We don't do it that way. We cut the stalks in the field and bring it back to the mill, then pull the fodder off, 'cause you generally have more people around the mill, and you can get more help. You can use the fodder and head for cow or chicken feed. You save your seed to plant with next year, and do that year after year. I think the modern type—hybrid or whatever—doesn't make as good of cane as the old kind. I've got some seed that's been in the family eighty years.

It's an all-day job to make it, and the more help you have, the better. It's hot work, done at a hot time of year. The reward is, that you get to taste it when it's done, and the kids especially look forward to that!

Alvin Chandler
page 72

Over the past three years my brothers and I have remodeled probably thirty or forty houses back in these mountains. We put new bathrooms and septic tanks in, fix up kitchens, do whatever people want. I'm here today to help Amos jack the low end of the house up. It's gettin' old and rotted out and we're going to put some new beams under it. We usually try to get to the job early and get a good jump on it, then sit down for lunch, visit a spell, then head back to work. We'll knock off late afternoon, pack up our tools, and head back to the house to finish up our chores there before dark if we can.

If you come to this house for a meal, you're in for good eatin'. Amos and Virgie won't let you go away hungry, that's for sure. There ain't nothin' like it. Mealtime is the highlight of the day when you come to work here!

Toney Plemmons
page 75

I growed up on my grandpap Keeners' land down here on Meadow Fork. 'Course I was pretty small over there. There was thirteen of us kids, and I wasn't the youngest. My dad moved us to Arkansas to homestead land when I was six. He didn't stay a year—he just made one crop. We raised cotton there in that bottomland, and picked it by hand. It was a dry year and they didn't know how to farm that county. They'd never grown cotton or nothing like that. There was a drought there that year, and the land just burned up. Food was hard to come by, and we didn't have a lot to eat. My dad had shipped a thirty gallon wooden barrel of molasses on the train with us going out. Them molasses sure come in handy. We moved back after that year. He laid it on my mother, but he was as dissatisfied as my mother was. Otherwise we was raised here, over from the church in the next hollow.

This cabin was probably built around 1850, and originally set up in the field, near the spring. Later they moved it down here near the creek. It's a story and a half tall, with a sleeping loft upstairs and a plank kitchen added on. It was built of hand-hewn logs. The lower rounds are poplar, some nineteen or twenty inches across. The top two or three rounds are made of chestnut. The top log is the wall plate log—it has round holes bored in it and they drove square pegs in them to hold the wall to it.

My wife, Edith, and I moved over here to this cabin in 1935. We rent the property and just pay a flat rate and get to keep whatever we make on it— tobacco, corn, pasture and all. My rent isn't all that much, maybe three or four hundred dollars a year for the whole farm. We hadn't planned to stay long, but we've been here ever since. Except for that year in Arkansas, I've lived within four or five miles of this one place all my life, and I'm eighty-six.

Clarence Ramsey
page 76

There was a man who lived up the hollow from us who had to come by our house on his way to cross the mountain. My father died when I was three years old and this fellow, Lumpy Norton, would stop by on his way to the store see if my mother needed anything. We all called him Uncle Lumpy.

I remember him coming by one day with his rig. I was about eight or nine years old at the time. He had a fine looking wagon and a big red mule. My mother gave him a five-dollar bill and a couple of ones to buy things we needed. After he left, us kids

started walking to school. On the way up a rocky section near some pine trees along the ridge, I saw a man's purse lying on the ground. It was a long pouch with a clip on the top. I picked it up and walked fast to get ahead of the other kids so I could look inside it and them not see. You know how kids act. There were about fifteen others that lived up the different hollers, and I didn't want them taking it from me.

When I got home that night, I gave the purse to my mother. I thought I'd get half the money for finding it, 'cause at least twenty-five wagons passed that way each day, and who knew whose purse it was. My mother looked through it and found a tax receipt with Uncle Lumpy's name on it. I knew the turnip was cooked then, and I'd not get a thing.

That evening Uncle Lumpy came back and you could see him walking beside his wagon looking this way and that along the road. When he got to the house he told my mother "this is the worst day of my life." She asked him what was wrong and he told her he'd lost all the money he had in the world. I had looked in the purse and knew the only money in it was what my mother had given him. She just let him talk on a bit, and then she told him "Uncle Lumpy, Clarence found your purse today." She wore an apron over her dress like women did back then. She had it in her dress pocket, under her apron, all the time.

He had bought the stuff my mother had asked for though. He bought it "on time." He was as honest as the day is long and he could get anything he wanted like that on time. He went to church every Sunday, year round, no matter what—rain, snow, or dead of winter—and every time he saw me from then on he thanked me for finding his purse. As I got older, that meant more to me than any reward money.

Homer Reeves
page 77

I can remember when there wasn't a foot of paved road between here and Asheville, and that's about twenty miles. Even with a good team of horses it was a full day's trip, and you didn't come back the same day—you stayed in Asheville. I would stay in my wagon at the livery stable. I wasn't the only one either—there were plenty of fellows that couldn't afford a place for the night, and would stay in the livery, or in someone's barn.

I used to go to town several times a year, to buy a little fertilizer or to sell a wagonload of tanbark. We would cut down chestnut oaks and then strip the bark and sell it to the tanneries. You would do anything for a dollar back then. A dollar was as big as a wagon wheel.

Dempsey Woody
page 78

You can never outthink a bear. They're a lot smarter than some people think. Now, I can tell about where we might jump one because I know their habits. They love white and red oak nuts and you can go to where these types of trees grow. Once you find a bear though, you'll try to figure which way he'll go and he'll go the other way every time. You think he'll go through a certain gap in the moun-

tains and he'll double back and slip through somewhere else.

When you're huntin' one you never want to get below him. You always want to shoot even with him, or from above where he is. I've seen 'em leap twelve feet at a bound even uphill and if you're below 'em, they can be on you before you know it. You have to really watch out once they're shot—they get really mean and can kill dogs before you can ever get up with them. I remember one old big bear that never would run, though. He went out in an open field and the fellows had automatic rifles firing at him. They didn't hit him a single shot and he didn't run even with all the shooting. The dogs got after him and he killed three, seriously wounded two or three others, and hurt three of four more before he was ever brought down. The old ones like that are smart. They've got to be to live to be that old. You can never predict what they'll do.

You've got to hunt with a bear club to get many bear. You need lots of dogs and men 'cause there's so many ways a bear can go in these mountains. One man just can't do it by himself. A bear on the run will take you through laurel thickets and some of the roughest country he can find. If you don't have enough men to cut him off, he'll get away from you every time. Of course it'd take all the sport out of it if you got one every time, but even with a club you'll only get one or two a year, and there's not many clubs any more.

I've been hunting since I was old enough for my daddy to help me over a log. I love to hunt, but mainly I just love getting out in the mountains, walking through the woods, and listening to the dogs way off barking, and picking out the sound of mine among the bunch.

Dempsey Woody
page 79

The female here had a litter of ten pups last time. She has a hot nose. She'll pick up a bear trail that's fresh and follow it on out. The male has a cold nose. He can pick up a trail that's two or three days old. He doesn't know what the word "quit" means. I've seen him follow a bear day and night for two

days. He'll run during the day and walk at night. The bear will walk, too. He doesn't want to get caught, but he can tell how close the dog is. The dog doesn't want to catch him by himself because he knows there's nothing he can do without other dogs but get in trouble, but he won't quit.

My father told me he'd heard of dogs picking up a trail that was three days old. I don't know if you'll believe this or not, but this male picked up on a trail that I know was seven days and seven nights old. He wanted to follow it, but I had him on a chain and didn't let him. I'd never seen him again if I had. The big male here is seven years old. I used him to catch groundhogs last summer, to keep him in practice for bear. He tickled me to death the way he went after one old big one. He went after him just like he would a bear—just circled and circled him until he found his chance, then he'd dice in and bite him. He never let up. That old groundhog got so mad he couldn't stand it. The dog was just too quick.

I've started dogs hunting when they were eleven months old, but you usually wait till they're about a year and a half. If you start one too little, and it goes up against a bear, it'll get buffaloed and never go up against one again. They should be big enough to run with the rest of the dogs and learn from them. I don't like to run my dogs two days in a row. They need a rest or their paws swell up and they get worn out. They need a day or two between chases.

My dogs are registered. Some people mix other breeds in with their dogs. Some mix a little bulldog with 'em, but if it's got too much bulldog in it, it will latch onto a bear and won't let go and you're going to lose your dog. The bear's going to kill it.

Bulldogs are like that; they get a hold of something and won't let go. A lot of dogs get killed every year by bear.

Bear hunting's one of the most expensive sports there is, I think. First you've got to have a four-wheel drive vehicle. You need all kinds of clothes, too, 'cause you never know what kind of weather you're going to run into. And you've got to have plenty of gas for all the riding around you have to do. Then you need a gun and some dogs. A good bear dog will run you around seven hundred dollars. If you pay two or three hundred for one, he won't stay the course. I lost two of the four I had this year. One died from some cause and the other one was either killed by a bear or stolen by somebody. Last I saw of him he was swimmin' across the river after a bear.

Rex Meadows
page 80

Kevin's learning to hunt with the rest of our bear club. He did real well this morning. He stayed right with us all the way, and we probably walked five or six miles over these mountains, through pretty rough country.

He's learning the safe way to hunt and the proper way to handle a gun—the same type of things my father taught my brother and me.

Bob Roberts
page 81

It looks like we're in for a rough winter this year, if the weather so far is any indication. I remember one snow back in March 1935 or '36. March twelfth it was. Boy, that was some snow! It started and kept it up day and night for three days. When it quit we had between four and five feet of snow on the ground. I had stacks of brush as high as a fence post stacked up around the farm, and after it quit snowing you couldn't see the brush or the fence post anymore! The horses would try to jump from place to place, they couldn't walk it was so deep.

Mrs. Marler
page 83

My grandfather was thrown away when he was just a baby. His mother took him, still wrapped in a diaper, and dumped him out of the wash pail, across a log, and right into a briar bush. A couple that didn't have no children, old man Bobby Payne and his wife, found him and took him in. They raised him like he was their own. Years later they found old man Payne's wife murdered. Everyone said her husband killed her, but no one could ever prove it. He took my grandfather and moved away.

When my grandfather was grown, he moved back there. Our family stayed with him about three months when I was growing up, but we couldn't stand living there. The place was haunted. Most nights you wouldn't hear or see a thing, but on dark nights you could see a kind of a spirit or something. It took the form of a bright blue light, like a rainbow, and would shine in and dance on the floor. It could open a latched door, and you would fasten the door back and it'd come right back loose. Other nights you could hear it go round the house and it would sound like someone was throwing chains or gears from a harness up on the porch. Sometimes you could hear it flopping around under the floorboards of the cabin.

One night it rattled and rattled the front door. The door didn't come open, but when my grandfather cursed the thing, it got riled and sounded like it'd dropped a stove on the roof. Then there was a rattling like chains all around the outside of the house. There was four inches of snow on the ground, but when they went outside to see what was going on, there wasn't even a cat or dog track showing. We packed up and left the next day, and even though I loved my grandfather, I never wanted to go back to that place again.

That's the biggest tale I've ever told, but every bit of it's the truth.

John Kilpatrick
page 84

When I was a younger man, just gettin' married, most people had already quit slaughtering their own hogs. They started taking them to the slaughterhouses. Dad had always done his own, and I decided to keep up the tradition, at least for a while. My father told me, "When the leaves get off the trees in the fall, and the creeks turn cold, and you've had your second frost, you can kill your hog and everything will be alright." He never lost a piece of meat following that advice, and none ever went bad on him.

The old timers used to wait until a hog got four or five hundred pounds before they'd kill them, but I think they're too hard to work with when they get that big. The one we're doing today is a little small. It's probably about 250 pounds. We're just doing the one today. We killed five hogs on Thanksgiving Day. Of course we had more help. I've even seen the day we did twelve.

The old folks used to use every part for something. They'd eat almost everything, including feet, ears, brains, and snout. Other parts were used for all sorts of things around the farm, including making kick balls for the kids. Even the fat was cooked and rendered out into lard, and also used to make soap.

When you shoot one, you make an imaginary "X" and aim between the eye and the ear. I try to do it with one shot. Then you cut his jugular vein and bleed him. He'll kick around a bit so you got to make sure there's nothing in his way, or it can break its leg and ruin a ham. Before you kill your hog you build a big fire under a fifty-five gallon drum and fill it with water. When it gets to almost boiling, you dip out the water into another drum and lower the slaughtered hog into it. After a bit you lift him out and start scraping the hair off. The hot water makes it easier to scrape the hair off, but if you leave it in too long, or the water is too hot, the hair will set up and you can't scrape it off. You have to cut it off with a razor.

After he's scraped good you cut off the head, split him down the stomach, and gut him. Next you split him down the backbone and hang the two halves in the smokehouse until the body heat gets out. When he's cooled down you can start salting and wrapping up the meat. As the water drains out of the body it draws the salt in and preserves the meat. You usually have to cure one at least two months, but you can start cutting bacon within a couple of weeks.

Today folks buy all their meat at the grocery store and don't even think about this part of it. They don't want to think how it got from the farm to their kitchen table. Somebody has to kill it, bleed it, boil off the hair, scrape it, gut it, and cut it up into hams and the like, then salt it and hang it up in the smokehouse. When you farm, you have to learn to do that all yourself, if you want to have bacon and sausage and ham for the winter.

McKinley "Doc" Caldwell
page 85

My parents started building this place in 1920. I remember they hired an eighty-four-year-old man to build the stone chimney. He used to get up at four in the morning and start to play his fiddle. The women folk would have to get up then, so he got his breakfast early and was up on the scaffolding by seven. He put down his tools for lunch at eleven and was back laying stone by noon. He would put his tools away for the day at four and go home. He worked for thirty-five cents an hour.

We lived seven miles from the river at Barnard and you had to cross the creek fourteen times to get up to our house. If it came a hard rain while you was away somewhere, you just had to sit on the bank and wait for the creek to go down again before you could go any further. The postman had the same problem come bad weather. He got fifty cents a day to deliver mail up this creek. Back then it only cost a few cents to mail a letter, and it took about a month to get anywhere.

I can remember the time when I was twelve and my sister Fanny and I laid off and planted a field of corn that yielded three hundred bushels, and my daddy never set a foot in the field. Fanny was a big girl then, maybe seven or eight years old. Now that's the way we were raised. I was nineteen before my family ever got a horse. Up to then I used mules and oxen to work the farm. I've worked hard all my life. I'm eighty-three years old now and I can still chop all my own firewood and do most of the chores that need doing around here.

Ernest Rector
page 87

When I was younger, I used to stay up with people all night when they were sick. I've gone three weeks on end, sleeping during the day and sitting up all night to watch after somebody. Most folks couldn't afford all the doctors and hospitals like they have today. Even when people died, they didn't take them to a mortician like they do today. They'd call somebody out to the house to prepare the body. That's what I used to do.

You could count on your friends and neighbors to give you a helping hand if you need it. I remember once, when Bill Taylor was sick, a bunch of us went over to his place and shucked and put up seven hundred bushels of corn so his hogs would have something to eat during the winter. We never got a penny for it, and didn't expect it either. We were glad to help out and knew we could count on others to do the same for us if we needed it. That was an everyday thing a few years back. Today, if you were dying of thirst, you couldn't get a man to give you a drink of water for less than a dollar.

Mr. Henderson
page 88

My father used to be the church secretary here in Walnut. He kept a record book that told how much the collection was each week. Cash money was hard to come by back then. Out of a congregation of about 100 to 150 people they would average about forty cents each week. He even wrote down who gave the most. It was usually the doctor. He'd give three or four cents every Sunday.

The Methodist Church was the biggest back then. All the funerals were held there, no matter who died. That old tree that stands in front of it has been that big as long as I can remember. No telling how old it is. It was that big even when I was a boy. Now the church isn't used much at all. It's mostly Freewill Baptist everywhere now. There's one of them churches around every bend it seems like.

Rev. Kenneth Parker
page 89

If the rest of the world saw us now, standing here in this freezing water, they'd probably think we were crazy, but I believe it doesn't matter what time of the year it is when a soul is saved—be it November or July. When my grandfather was baptized, it was the dead of winter, and they had to break the ice to do it. He was ninety-seven years old then but it didn't bother him none. He didn't get sick afterwards or anything. I've done a lot of baptizing, praise the Lord, but I've never heard of anyone getting sick from it no matter what time of year it was. You see if you do something for the Lord, He'll take care of you.

I believe the Bible teaches baptism, and I'm thankful to be a part of it. The Lord was baptized in the Jordan and I believe in doing it as close to the Bible as you can. Most churches today have pools in them, and it doesn't matter a bit regarding your salvation where it's done and it's none of my business, but folks here had a vote on it and decided not to build an inside pool, and I'm glad they did, God bless them.

Some of the men from the church came in here yesterday with a backhoe and made us a pool in this creek next to the church. So here we are today, baptizing these young folks in the name of the Lord, in these cold November waters. None of us knows how long we're on this earth. We may die tomorrow or the Lord may come for us today. There's no time to waste.

Ernest Teague
page 90

When I was a boy my father had a horse he used to deliver the mail. One Sunday morning we were out washing and currying him, gettin' him all cleaned up, and the preacher came by. He asked if we were coming to church and my father told him that he reckoned not, as we had a lot to do around the house. The preacher looked at him and said, "Well, I'll tell you what, you just stand there and curry your way right to hell." Then he turned and rode off. My

father thought on that a few minutes and said, "Son, let's go to the house and get cleaned up. We need to be in church this morning." And we went, too!

Alma Ferguson
page 91

My brother-in-law Bud was on his tractor, on that steep hill up beside my house. He had a chain around an old log and was trying to pull it up the hill. I guess he'd done the same thing a dozen times before, but it'd been raining and the ground was soaked. The wheels slid in the mud, and the tractor reared up and knocked him off. Then it turned over on him. I was looking out my window and saw it happen. We called the emergency folks, but he was already gone. He couldn't have suffered long.

I'm so glad they're burying him here at the Oak Hill Cemetery. He loved his church and all the folks in it. The men came in this morning and dug the grave by hand. The women are bringing in a meal, to share with everyone after the service.

He'll really be missed, but he's gone on to a better place—to be with our Lord.

Mr. Henderson
page 92

This place used to be called Jewel Hill before they changed the name to Walnut. Before that I heard that it was called Duel Hill because two fellows had a duel up here and one was killed. I guess it was just through confusion that it came to be called Jewel

Peggy Harmon
page 93

Hill. It stayed that way until the post office came in, then they changed the name to Walnut because I think there was already another Jewel Hill somewhere.

Walnut used to be the county seat and was a fair-size little community. An old frame schoolhouse used to set just to the right of where the Missionary Baptist Church sits today. The brick schoolhouse here was built around 1933. My grandfather told me about a "whipping block" that sat next to where the Walnut supply store is now. For punishment they would fasten a man's arms and legs in it and whipped him. Either the sheriff or the justice of the peace did it.

I used to love to hear stories about the way things were. I remember many a night as a boy, falling asleep in front of the fire listening to my father and some of our neighbors talk about their experiences in the Spanish-American War. My grandfather fought in the Civil War and I remember him talking about that, too. I still remember some of his stories.

When I was young, that mountain to the right of the Walnut School, over in Doe Branch, used to be bald on top. It was just old "slatey" dirt. There weren't any trees at all, no brush or plants either. The old folks used to tell us it was a volcano and that it could erupt at any time. All us kids believed it, too, and we ran around scared half the time that it was going to blow up! Stories like that made a big impression on our small minds.

The government came in later and did something to make things grow and planted pine trees up there. It's all covered with trees now, but you can still tell where the new growth starts.

Aunt Alice was eighty-nine last April. She never married but she lives here in the big house by herself next to Momma and Daddy, and my husband and I, and we keep an eye on her. She started feeling bad a couple of weeks ago. We took her to the doctor and he gave us some medicine to give her. She was fine until last Wednesday. I began to notice things—like her dropping her matches all over the floor while she was trying to light a fire. She got to feelin' real bad and we had to put her to bed.

She's gone through four stages so far. At first she would just lie in her bed and wouldn't talk. She wouldn't answer anybody, no matter what they asked her. Then she began to talk to me, and next she talked all day. She said funny things you know. She was seeing things that weren't there and imagining all sorts of things. Then she started getting violent. She'd talk back mean to us and hit at us when we got near her. She kept kicking around in bed—she thought she was walking I guess.

We finally got her calmed down and today she's fine. I hope she'll stay this way and get better. Momma watches her during the day while I'm at work, and I stay with her at night. If you have the right medicine and know what's wrong with them, I think you can take good care of someone at home. I know she's happier here than she'd be in the hospital. She's in her own bed, all her friends come to visit, and she's surrounded by family, not strangers.

Bud Norton
page 94

People can't spend time with anybody anymore. They're always in a hurry, and gettin' up and goin'.

146

They've always got to be somewhere else. Back when I was young, folks would come over on Sunday afternoon to visit. The women would talk, and do whatever in the house, and the men would sit out in the yard and whittle on a big log. Five or six of them would sit on that big log whittlin' for hours passin' the time and swappin' stories. After they'd leave you could pick up enough shavings to build a fire with. People don't do that anymore. Seems like they don't have the time they used to.

Mrs. Lockie Coates
page 95

When we have baptisms and homecomings at the church, it's too far for some of the congregation to go home to eat and get back for the services, so we just have everything spread out here. Everybody just fixes a dish and brings it to church.

We'll have things going on all day. Folks will come to the morning services and after it's over we'll spread out all the food on tables and everyone shares. Then we'll have a baptizing down at the creek and gospel singing in the afternoon. Later we go up to the top of the hill to the church cemetery and put flowers on the graves. At dinner everyone eats what's left of the food, has some dessert and coffee, and then attends the evening sermon.

It's nice to have your friends and family around you, spend the day with them, and get a chance to talk and visit and catch up on things. The young folks enjoy it, too, and the kids get to play with their friends. Of course everybody in our church is related in some way it seems, so there's a special bond of love here, too.

Byard Ray
page 97

Before there was television and radio, the mountain folk had to provide their own entertainment. They learned to sing, dance, and make music. Whenever there was a barn raising or a get-together at harvest time, or any special event, the people would go get whatever instrument out that they could play, find a favorite tune they all knew, and start up. The others would clog dance or sing along.

I first learned to play the fiddle when I was just a boy of six or seven. My father played the fiddle and used to keep it hanging up on the wall when he wasn't playing it. My brother and I were warned not to touch it, but I wanted to play it so bad that I would get it down and try it when my parents weren't around. I had to promise my little brother that he could play with any of my toys, if he wouldn't tell on me.

There was an old doctor who would travel around the mountains visiting all the farms, and one day he came to our house when my brother and I were the only ones home. He took down the fiddle and played it while he waited on them to get back. When he finished my brother told him I could play, too. He asked me to show him, and was surprised how well I could do it. When my mother got back he told her, and she got a switch down and started after me, 'cause I'd been told not to touch it. The doctor got in between her and me, and told her if she switched me he wouldn't come back no more. He made her listen to me, and pretty soon she was clogging on the kitchen floor.

I played in festivals and won all sorts of awards later on, and my fiddle even took me to Mexico, Canada, and to England. I even went out to Hollywood, California, to be in a movie. When I'm gone for long though, I get homesick and my mind goes back to growing up on the farm, and to when I was a boy and would walk along a cow trail after a rain and feel the mud between my toes. Funny what things your mind remembers from when you were young.

Kate Church
page 98

My father served five years during the great Civil War. He told me there was times when he laid his blanket down for the night on top of a foot of snow, with a dead man within an arms length on each side of him. They had to scrounge for any food they could find. He said that sometimes food was so scarce they had to kill rats and eat them. They would stop at farms along the way and be so hungry, and have so little time before they moved on, that they would kill a hog and not even be able to cook it long enough to be safe to eat, but they ate it anyway or they'd starved.

When he died there wasn't even a car around—only trains. What roads there were, was meant for

wagons, and were built along old cow trails. Later, when they built roads for cars, every man had to work one week a year on a road crew, or pay someone to work in his stead.

When I was a girl we raised sheep to make clothing, cows for milk, chickens for eggs, and hogs to slaughter. We kept the eggs and milk in the creek to keep them cold. We grew all our food on the farm. There weren't no stores nearby then, not even a mill to grind the wheat for a long time. What you didn't grow or raise you didn't have. We used to take a wooden sled to town about once a year to get coffee and sugar and such, and we traded for that. My mother would spin wool to make yarn for our clothes. Us kids would sit and pull burrs out for her. I did that up until I was growed, and then I learned how to spin.

I'm not sure how old I am. Somewheres between ninety-two and a hundred I reckon. When I was married in 1910, my husband registered me as being twenty-two, but I think I was older. I raised seven children. All of them was born at home and most of them without any midwife to help—there weren't many of them around then, and we hardly ever saw a doctor in these parts.

Lewis Roberts
page 99

I was born in Craggy and moved here to Alexander when I was a boy. My daddy lived here until he died out. I stayed on. He and I used to log a lot over on Little Pine Creek. We were over there when the big tornado hit back it the thirties. The church there was picked up and turned around and set down across the street from where it was. One man was even killed there.

I've been around wood all my life. We used to cut it and haul the logs down to the French Broad River. Some of the logs were so big we would have to hook up two mules, with four oxen behind them, to pull them. We'd put them in and they'd catch them out on down the river, and take them to the sawmill.

We'd cut firewood to sell, too. It would take two good hands a long day to cut a cord of wood and then we'd get four dollars to split for it. We even sold cords of pulpwood to Champion Paper. We'd have to strip the bark off by hand before they'd take it. We cut white pine and sold it for five dollars a thousand board feet. Even at that they wouldn't accept anything with knots. Back then wood wasn't worth anything. There's been so much wood cut out of here over the past fifty years, that the mills will take anything they can get now.

We also used to clear new ground for folks. We'd work for twenty dollars an acre and that'd average out to about fifty cents to a dollar a day. Of course the dollar was worth more in those days. Today, if you go anywhere, you'd better take a tote sack full of money or you'll run out.

Zola Payne
page 101

I think fall is one of the prettiest times of year here. These old mountains just turn to a blaze of color. All the beautiful colored leaves look like a quilt on the ground when they fall off. You feel the first nip in the air of the morning, and you know summer's gone and winter's coming on. They'll be lots more chores to do—wood to cut and put up, canning to finish up, stores to lay away. Lots to get ready before bad weather sets in.

I think it's one of the loneliest times, too. When the leaves are gone, and the trees are left bare, it seems like loneliness sets in. You know winter is coming on, and people won't be getting out as much to visit.

Homer Reeves
page 102

When I left home for the service back in World War I, my girlfriend gave me a red-letter edition of the Bible to carry with me. I kept it all through the war. When I got home, I was put in the military hospital down in Charleston to recover from exposure to mustard gas. After a bit, a buddy and I decided we were well enough to leave, but the doctors kept saying "a few more days."

We didn't want to wait any longer so we borrowed two fellows' dress uniforms, snuck out, and headed home. We ran all the way to the railway station. Our train was pullin' out when we got there and we had to chase it down the track. We grabbed hold of the caboose car, and pulled ourselves aboard. It didn't go past Spartanburg, so we slept on benches at the station that night and caught the first train to Asheville the next day.

I found a fellow with a team of horses and wagon who was headed to Spring Creek, so I hooked up with him. He gave me a ride as far as he could, but it'd been raining a lot and the wagon kept miring up, so I lit out on foot across the mountain.

I dragged in home about one A.M. Everyone was in bed so I lit some matches and made my way upstairs to my brother's bedroom. I crawled in my bunk and slept solid all night. The next morning I got up early and went downstairs to where my mother was fixing breakfast in the kitchen. She had her back to me and was rolling some biscuits in flour. She thought I was my brother and talked to me about five or ten minutes. When I never did say nothing, she finally turned around. She was so surprised she screamed and flour flew off her hands and all over me. She was so happy to see me she grabbed me and I thought she would never stop crying. When she finally let me go, I was covered with flour from head to toe!

After I'd been home a few days my girlfriend and I decided to get married. We've been together ever since. I thought back later about the Bible she'd given me, and realized in my hurry to get home I'd left it lying on my hospital bunk back in Charleston. I regretted losing it after carrying it all that time, but I guess it did me good when I needed it the most, and it sure was a comfort during those awful days of the war.

until he hurt himself unloading a threshing machine. He got dizzy and had to lay down, the other men said. The next day he went up to spray our tobacco for bugs and he got sick. He thought it was the spray, but found out later he had busted something inside that caused a blood clot and tumor to form in his brain. He went blind for two years and deaf for six months before he died. That was fifty-two years ago last April.

I've worked all my life. I could get food stamps and such, but I don't. I think half the people today live off the government. I'm like a squirrel I guess. I still put away a few things for the winter no matter how old I get. I don't can much food anymore, but I still freeze quite a bit. It's less trouble and quicker than canning. When people didn't have electricity and such they had to can things. Now that's all changing.

I'm eighty-eight now and I don't imagine I'll live to see eighty-nine. I'm not worried though. I've lived a clean life, never lied, never stole nor cheated, and I haven't associated myself with trash. The Lord will rise in the east and when Gabriel blows his trumpet it won't scare me a bit. I'm expecting it and I'm ready.

Bertha Marler
page 103

Myrtle's my oldest daughter. She lives with me now. She's an old maid—she's never been married. Her father died when she was fourteen and she had to quit school to take care of the younger kids so I could go to work to support us. My husband was forty-one years old when he died. He'd never been sick a day in his life. He was the picture of health

Ernest Teague
page 104

I was in the mill business for most of my life. Back in 1939, when I was manager at the A&P, a banker fellow in Marshall came by and asked if I would be interested in takin' over a mortgage on a mill they had taken back. I thought about it a spell, then told 'em I would. They set me up on a time payment plan.

Things were goin' good till the big flood of 1941 hit. The river came up out of its banks and flooded most of the businesses in town. The water got halfway up the walls of my buildin' before it stopped. Everythin' was under water or floatin' around. It was all ruined. I still owed on the buildin', and had payments to make or I'd lose it, too. I dug in, cleaned the place up, and got back on my feet. I worked twice as hard to get things goin' again. I'd go to the train station at night, unload bags of fertilizer, feed, seed, and supplies, put them on my truck, and drive them back to the mill, to restock everythin'. It took three hard years to get back on solid ground.

For over forty years I ground corn and wheat for area farmers to make flour, corn meal, grits and hominy. I sold veterinary items, horse and dog food, and supplies needed for growin' tobacco. I loved every minute of it and thanked God for the blessin's of good health, a bit of business sense, and the support of the local folks. My business was an important one to the community and I enjoyed what I did. I made a lot of friends there over the years, too. A man can't ask for much more than that!

Aunt Laura Cook
page 105

I came here to the Gahagan home in 1906, when I was just fifteen years old, to help Lilly Gahagan care for her brother's turkeys. He was known as "old man Wade Gahagan," and was going to be gone for a few weeks on business. I also helped out with the housework and anything that needed doin' around this place. I stayed on for years, then moved away and got married. I raised five children of my own. When my husband died twenty-two years ago,

young Wade Gahagan's wife asked me to come back and help take care of her boys. They all call me "Aunt Laura," though I'm not blood related to them. I don't work for them anymore, but I still live here and have a room in what was the old slave quarters.

The turkeys used to roost in this tree when I first came here. I would climb up in it and shake the limbs to get them down. It was a lot smaller then and I was a lot younger. That old tree has changed a lot in my lifetime. It's gotten bigger and stronger and I've gotten smaller and weaker! I'm ninety-one now and can't climb it no more.

Lloyd Rigsby
page 106

I was born on May 14th, 1900. When I was nineteen I nearly died of the flu epidemic. They say I stayed in bed for three weeks, flat on my back, and I was unconscious most of that time. Doctors were even afraid of it. They didn't know what to do — just couldn't figure it out. Old Doc Moore came to see me once. I didn't get any better after his visit so they sent word for him to come again. He cursed and told them, "I'm not about to back up there near that flu!"

My two brothers got it, too. Fortunately my father and stepmother never took it. They spent day and night lookin' after us boys, never known' if we'd live or die.

Even after I started to get better I couldn't walk forty feet to the mailbox without having to stop two or three times to rest. It felt like my legs were going to give out from under me. I could run my hand through my hair and bring out a handful by the roots. I guess the high fever just killed it. It never grew back. My father, at eighty-nine, had more hair than I did when I was twenty.

I've heard that more folks died of that flu than they did in the whole of the First World War, and most of them were the younger, healthy folks that you'd think would be the last to get it.

Bud Norton
page 107

There's not a man back in this country that's worked any harder than I have in my life. I'll be eighty come this summer, if I live that long. I've put five children through school, supported my family, and built up this place. It's been a hard life. A fellow just about needs to be married out here. Not much way to make much for yourself if you're not. It takes two people workin' all the time and then it's still not easy.

My wife and I have been married forty-seven years, going on forty-eight. We've raised two boys and three girls here. My wife comes from a big family, too. She's got eleven brothers and sisters and they're all still living. So is her father. When people get old they need other folks around—close in if they can—so when my boy told me he wanted to build a place, I told him he could have a parcel of my land. He said he'd just as soon do that as build anywhere else. A fellow's family is about all he can count on. They're about the best help he can get.

Children can be a lot of trouble, too, that's for sure, but I guess they're worth it. I had an old uncle, he's dead now, but he used to say that when kids are little they tromp all over your feet and when they get older they tromp all over your heart. He sure knew what he was talking about. But I love little kids, I'm just crazy about them. I enjoy my own, too. They

come and help out ever chance they get. I can't get around like I used to, so they helped me put up my tobacco this year. I don't know what I'd done without 'em.

We also still use animals a lot around the farm. I've had my horse, Kate, for eleven years now. She was born right here in my barn. I've worked many a field with her—tobacco, or whatever I had. I plow up a lot of times with a tractor now, but I still use her to tend the fields. She's the only thing I got that's not for sale. A man came up here one time and asked me what I wanted for a dog. It was sick and all and I told him I wouldn't have to have more than a quarter for him. He took him, too. Took him at that price and I had to stick to my word. Another man came up here and asked about Kate. I told him fifteen hundred dollars wouldn't touch her because she's not for sale. There's not any amount of money that can buy her. She means the world to me.

Collie Payne
page 109

I've raised Berry from a calf and he's sixteen now. I trained him to plow and have turned crops with him for the past fourteen years. I've worked mules, too, but the doctor told me to slow down a bit and take it easy, so I use Berry now. I never have to raise my voice to him. I just give him a command and he does it. I guess we've worked so much together all these years he knows what I want without me even telling him. I plow with him and he pulls a sled. I use him to help clear fields and such, too. He's slower to work than a mule but he's more surefooted, and you need that on this kind of mountain land. I don't know what I'd do without him now.

John Chandler
page 110

Charlie Thomas
page 111

I've raised gamecocks for over twenty years. I have pens set up behind my house, and keep each cock in a separate one. My father raised and fought them, too, and he taught me what he knew. I keep accurate records on all the cocks, just like breeders of other animals do. I have records on the great-grandfathers of some of these cocks. I can tell you how they were bred, when they were hatched, how many brothers they had, and how many fights they have fought. Each year I experiment a little in breeding my own. You're always looking for the right combination that makes a winning fighting cock. I have nearly ten ready to fight right now, depending on the size of the derby.

We've always taken the best care in raising them. I grind all my own food. I get most of the ingredients at the health food store—wheat, corn, cod liver oil, and such. I think it's best if you stay with nature, rather than buying the premixed stuff.

You know people call cockfighting inhumane, but the best way I know to explain it, is that we raise them good, feed and take care of them properly, and match them up by weight before we fight them. There's never more than two ounces difference in their weight between the cocks that are fighting. Then we just put them in the ring together and let them do what comes natural. If you put two cocks together in a barnyard they'd fight just the same, till one of them was dead, and it'd be a lot bloodier than when we fight them in a derby. Their natural spurs make for a much worse fight than with the metal spurs we put on them. Our animals are important to us, and we take good care of them.

I wish you had been around when my uncle was still alive. Boy, he could have told you some stories. He used to work at a sawmill up on the mountain toward Hot Springs. He would walk six or seven miles each way from Little Laurel to work and then have to put in a ten-hour day. He would leave home about four in the morning and have to be to work and have the boiler fired up by the time the rest of the men got there. It was a steam-run saw mill and the boiler built up the steam that turned the saw. There were plenty of big trees to cut back then. Even when I was a boy, I can remember walking across many a stump six and seven foot across.

My father cut wood in the Laurel area, too, and cut the biggest poplar in these parts. They got several thousand board feet up to the first branch. There was a chestnut tree I heard about that you could take a ten-foot rod inside, and turn it around, and never touch the sides. A couple lived in the hollow of that tree until they got their house built.

My father used to walk ten miles to work and back every day to cut wood. He got paid about a dollar fifty a day. They would haul it down to the railroad and load it onto cars, and send it to Stackhouse where they had a big band saw to cut it up with. Old man Wade Gahagan owned the sawmill. It was down near the river for a while, and then he moved it up on the mountain so it would be closer to where the timber cuttin' was going on. That was back in the 1920s. Now you can hardly find trees worth cuttin'.

Amy Edgins
page 112

I write country songs. I write about all sorts of stuff—the mountains, my life, things that happen around here, stuff like that. I've written over four hundred now, and I'm only sixteen. When I get a bunch done I send them down to the radio station in Marshall. I haven't heard anything back from them, but I hope somebody will record one some day. I just enjoy doing it though, and it means something to me, so it don't matter as much what other people think of them.

Wade Massey
page 114

I've lived here for more than thirty-five years. I lived in Detroit, Michigan, for a while when I found work up there. You couldn't give that place to me now though. Too much going on even when I was up there, and its probably gotten worse by now.

A lot of people from Florida and other places come to these mountains each year. None of 'em farm though. I guess they'd starve if they had to farm for a living. Back in these mountains you've got to do it all your life to make a go at it. It's year round work and even then it's hard to make it. They buy up the land because it's cheap compared to where they're from, but it makes the prices go up and means higher taxes for everybody else. They put up a house they'll only use for a few months in the summer, and then go back to where they came from. They even complain of the smell after you put fertilizer down, or if you have cattle in a field near where they're staying. Pretty soon farmers like us can't afford our own land anymore.

Evia Metcalf
page 115

I like livin' here. People have tried to get me to move, but I won't. It gets a little crazy with the young folks though. Last Saturday night, a bunch of them were down at the house below me, raisin' a commotion. I thought they'd quiet down after a while, but at two o'clock in the morning they were still going at it. I hollered out of my window for them to settle down so I could get some sleep, but they wouldn't. I laid there awhile longer and then got my gun down and came out to the door. I told them to quiet down again, or I'd shoot. They didn't pay me no mind, so I let off a couple of shots. I tried to shoot at the treetops, but they all know I'm blind and can't see a bit no more, so boy, they cleared out then!

Amanda Gunter
page 116

Tammy is my first cousin. She's deaf and has to go to a special school away from here, down in Morganton. She comes to stay with us for a few weeks in the summer. When she visits, she teaches me sign language. I'm about the only one she can talk to around here. I know how to say anything I want, and now we talk all the time, and nobody else knows what we are talking about. I really love having her here.

B. W. Payne
page 117

When I was a boy, I used to slip away every chance I got and go talk to an old fellow who'd tell us kids stories about the Civil War times and such. He was too young to fight in the war, but his dad was of servin' age. The armies would come through the communities and take your food, horses, and anything else they needed, and there wasn't a thing you could do about it. Either army would make you join them if they found you. They had a big family to care for, so his father would hide out in the mountains, at the head of Little Pine Creek, when they came through. The old man told me he used to have to take food up to his father while he was hiding out, and leather so he could keep working, making shoes and such for the family to wear in the winter.

I'd go listen to the old man's stories whenever my father didn't have work for me to do. I'd sit for hours listening to him. He'd talk all day if you'd let him. Boy, he could really picture things to you, just as clear as if you were there. I was just a boy then and stories like that made a real big impression on me. They must have, 'cause I still remember them today.

GEORGE TICE is best known for his photographic vision of America and his finely crafted prints. He is author or twelve books including *George Tice, Selected Photographs, 1953–1999*; *Fields of Peace: A Pennsylvania German Album*; *Urban Landscapes*; *Lincoln*; and *Stone Walls and Grey Skies*. His prints can be found in the collections of the Museum of Modern Art and the Metropolitan Museum of Art, where, in 1972, he was honored with a one-man show. A major retrospective of his work, "Urban Landscapes," was held at New York's International Center of Photography in 2002.

TIM BARNWELL is a commercial and fine art photographer based in Asheville, North Carolina. His career has spanned over Twenty - five years as both a professional photographer and a photography instructor, including eight years as executive director of the nationally recognized school, Appalachian Photographic Workshops.

His images have been widely published, appearing in dozens of magazines including *Time, Newsweek, Southern Accents, House Beautiful, American Craft, Outdoor Photographer, Sky and Telescope, US Air, Blue Ridge Country, U.S. News and World Report, Billboard, Travel South, American Style, Black & White Magazine*, and *National Parks*.

Mr. Barnwell's fine art work has been included in dozens of group and one-man shows both in the United States and abroad, and is widely collected. His prints are in the permanent collections of The Metropolitan Museum of Art, The New Orleans Museum of Art, The High Museum in Atlanta, The Mint Museum in Charlotte, R.J. Reynolds Industries, The SOHO Photo Gallery in New York, and the Bank of America corporate collection.

SAM GRAY is a museum director, writer, and curator. He has spent his professional career using photographs to help interpret the culture and history of Western North Carolina. He served as Director of the Mountain Heritage Museum from 1978 to 1984, before joining North Carolina's Department of Cultural Resources as the Director of the Mountain Gateway Museum.

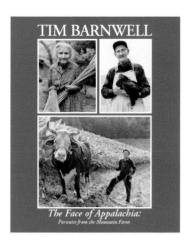

LIMITED EDITION HARDCOVER BOOKS, POSTERS

The Face of Appalachia is also available in limited and special editions. *The Face of Appalachia: Limited Edition*, consists of fifty numbered books, each signed by the author. The second version, *The Face of Appalachia: Special Edition* includes an autographed book with a correspondingly numbered and signed original photograph. The print, "Collie Payne and steer, Berry, in tobacco field" (cover photograph), is an 11 x 14-inch fiber based photograph mounted and matted on 16 x 20-inch museum board.

A 24 x 30-inch exhibit poster (shown above), with three photographic duotone reproductions, is also available from this series. For information, contact Numinous Editions, 244 Coxe Avenue, Asheville, NC 28801 or by email at numinouseditions@hotmail.com.

TRAVELING EXHIBITION AND PRINTS

A traveling exhibit of photographic prints, selected from images in this book, is available to galleries, museums, and universities. The show consists of thirty framed prints, but can be modified or expanded to meet the needs of the exhibitor. An information packet is available upon request.

Images reproduced in this book are also available as fine art photographic prints, and are offered in a variety of sizes. They are hand printed by the author, archivally processed, and mounted and matted on museum board.

For information on the exhibit or prints, galleries representing Mr. Barnwell's work, and the most current schedule of upcoming shows, visit the Web page www.barnwellphoto.com and follow the link to the fine art pages. Inquiries can also be directed to the author at barnwellphoto@hotmail.com.